Rural Workers, Sindicatos and Collective Bargaining in Rio Grande do Sul

"The development of this type of undertaking, of 'traveler-research', especially in the current context, is endowed with difficulty and substantial merit. The author shows that it is possible to build an academic narrative with rigor and, at the same time, one that is committed to the reader, rendering the text an experience of in-depth reflection and, also, an exciting read. This work will become an excellent research reference, one that is worthy of a place on the shelf of any bookstore section focused on rural work, unions and collective labor agreements"
—Ronaldo Bernardino Colvero, *Federal University of Pampa, Brazil*

"This book is certainly timely and goes right to the point, like an arrow. It's short and broad at the same time. This book could be useful for a broad audience to better understand hindrances to just labor practices and may help to overcome these challenges. Readers will be rewarded by a small, big book, and by following the endeavor that Davide Carbonai performed throughout the COVID-19 pandemic"
—Sergio Schneider, *Federal University of Rio Grande do Sul (UFRGS), Brazil*

"Davide Carbonai's book represents an important contribution to all those interested in debates about the world of work. One of the main contributions of Carbonai's book is that it develops this discussion in rural areas, giving voice to a group of workers who have had their lives organized based on activities in the countryside. It offers an especially interesting debate in the case of Brazil, where in recent years the sectors associated with agribusiness have become one of the main representatives of conservatism in the country"
—Alfredo Alejandro Gugliano, *Federal University of Rio Grande do Sul (UFRGS), Brazil*

Davide Carbonai

Rural Workers, Sindicatos and Collective Bargaining in Rio Grande do Sul

palgrave
macmillan

Davide Carbonai
Department of Administrative Sciences
Federal University of Rio Grande do Sul
Porto Alegre, Brazil

ISBN 978-3-030-94807-8   ISBN 978-3-030-94808-5 (eBook)
https://doi.org/10.1007/978-3-030-94808-5

© The Author(s), under exclusive licence to Springer Nature Switzerland AG 2022

This work is subject to copyright. All rights are solely and exclusively licensed by the Publisher, whether the whole or part of the material is concerned, specifically the rights of translation, reprinting, reuse of illustrations, recitation, broadcasting, reproduction on microfilms or in any other physical way, and transmission or information storage and retrieval, electronic adaptation, computer software, or by similar or dissimilar methodology now known or hereafter developed.

The use of general descriptive names, registered names, trademarks, service marks, etc. in this publication does not imply, even in the absence of a specific statement, that such names are exempt from the relevant protective laws and regulations and therefore free for general use.

The publisher, the authors and the editors are safe to assume that the advice and information in this book are believed to be true and accurate at the date of publication. Neither the publisher nor the authors or the editors give a warranty, expressed or implied, with respect to the material contained herein or for any errors or omissions that may have been made. The publisher remains neutral with regard to jurisdictional claims in published maps and institutional affiliations.

Cover pattern © Melisa Hasan

This Palgrave Macmillan imprint is published by the registered company Springer Nature Switzerland AG.
The registered company address is: Gewerbestrasse 11, 6330 Cham, Switzerland

To Marcello, Maria, Deise, and Pablo

Acknowledgments

I dare not imagine how many kilometers I traveled, far and wide, through the Serra, the central region and the Brazilian pampa of Rio Grande do Sul, interviewing, here and there, trade unionists and rural workers. I suppose it was a lot of hours spent in the car thinking and organizing ideas around a complex topic: a regional system of employment relations, with many actors involved, different levels of analysis and questionable working conditions.

I would like to thank those people who helped me in this research, especially those who granted me an interview: it is a long list, as you will see in the next chapters. Ultimately, this book would not have been possible were it not for the support of the Fetar (Federação do Trabalhadores Assalariados Rurais) who organized a series of meetings and facilitated my research.

Depending on the ongoing analysis of the interviews, I revised my initial hypotheses and redesigned the research several times. I hope this book will serve to elucidate a complex system of relationships among rural unions, in-work poverty and the legal system.

Contents

1 **Introduction**   1
   Theoretical Contributions   3
   Methodological Notes   6
   Plan of the Book   10
   References   10

2 **Rural Salaried Workers**   15
   Class Identity   16
   Safety at Work   24
   Getting a Job   30
   References   35

3 **Aspects of Rural Unionism**   37
   The Sindicatos de Trabalhadores Rurais   40
   Collective Bargaining   45
   Negotiating Clauses   48
   Providing Services   55
   References   59

4	**What Is a Rural Union for?**	61
	The COVID-19 Pandemic	62
	The Puzzle of Representation	64
	A Comparison	71
	References	74
5	**Final Considerations**	75
	There Is an Elephant in the Room	75
	The Crisis of Labor Representation	79
	References	83

References 87

Index 93

Abbreviations

CAGED	Cadastro Geral de Empregados e Desempregados (General Register of Employment and Unemployment)
CLT	Consolidação das Leis Trabalhista (Consolidation of Labor Law)
Contag	Confederação Nacional dos Trabalhadores na Agricultura (National Confederation of Agricultural Workers)
Contar	Confederação Nacional dos Trabalhadores Assalariados e Assalariados Rurais (National Confederation of Male and Female Rural Salaried Workers)
CTB	Central dos Trabalhadores e Trabalhadoras do Brasil (Central of Male and Female Workers of Brazil)
CUT	Central Única dos Trabalhadores (Central Union of Workers)
EC	Emenda Constitucional (Constitutional Amendment)
Farsul	Federação da Agricultura do Estado do Rio Grande do Sul (Federation of Agriculture of the State of Rio Grande do Sul)
Fetag	Federação do Trabalhadores da Agricultura (Federation of Agricultural Workers)
Fetar	Federação dos Trabalhadores Assalariados Rurais no Rio Grande Sul (Federation of Rural Salaried Workers in Rio Grande Sul)
Fetraf	Federação dos Trabalhadores na Agricultura Familiar (Federation of Workers in Family Farming)
ILO	International Labour Organization
INPC	Índice Nacional de Preços ao Consumidor (National Consumer Price Index)
INSS	Instituto Nacional do Seguro Social (National Institute of Social Security)
MP	Medida Provisória (Decree-Law)

MPT	Ministério Público do Trabalho (Public Ministry of Labor)
PEC	Projeto de Emenda Constitucional (Constitutional Amendment Proposal)
PNAD	Pesquisa Nacional por Amostra de Domicílios (National Household Sample Survey)
PT	Partido dos Trabalhadores (Workers Party)
STAF	Sindicato de Trabalhadores da Agricultura Familiar (Family Farming Workers' Union)
STR	Sindicato de Trabalhadores Rurais (Rural Workers' Union)
TSE	Tribunal Superior Eleitoral (Superior Electoral Court)
UPA	Unidade de Pronto Atendimento (Emergency Medical Care Unit)

LIST OF FIGURES

Fig. 1.1　Regions in Rio Grande do Sul　7
Fig. 3.1　Multiple correspondence analysis plot for dimensions 1 and 2 (categories)　49

CHAPTER 1

Introduction

Abstract Main theoretical contributions and research notes are presented in the first chapter. The author presents the socioeconomic context of Rio Grande do Sul. In this chapter, there are links to multimedia materials that are meant to accompany the reading of the book.

Keywords Theoretical contributions • In-depth interviews • Methodology • Rio Grande do Sul

This book is about rural wage workers and collective bargaining in Rio Grande do Sul (the southernmost state of Brazil). I am presenting the results of nearly two years of research, even though it was often interrupted due to COVID-19. In Brazil, and especially Rio Grande do Sul, there has been no pause in the COVID-19 crisis from March 2020 until the final draft of this book. For this reason, my research approach has been more pragmatic. Relationships with interviewees and data collection, specifically the negotiation of access to the field, have been revolutionized. I used different techniques—qualitative and quantitative—one after the other. I carried out face-to-face interviews during the first few months of 2020 and after June 2021, complying with necessary precautions of social

© The Author(s), under exclusive license to Springer Nature Switzerland AG 2022
D. Carbonai, *Rural Workers, Sindicatos and Collective Bargaining in Rio Grande do Sul*, https://doi.org/10.1007/978-3-030-94808-5_1

distancing and mask-wearing. Other interviews were conducted over the phone.

In Rio Grande do Sul, rural labor at the estâncias (over 3000 hectares in territorial extension) or in the smaller fazendas is a pathway out of extreme poverty for many rural wage workers (*assalariados rurais*). However, taking care of the cattle, planting rice, harvesting soy, drying tobacco leaves or picking fruit doesn't always guarantee an adequate living standard. This is the first reason why I decided to study the *assalariados*: an extremely low wage which is earned for a difficult, exhausting and even hazardous job.

In 2018, 1.48 million people in Rio Grande do Sul (13.1% of the total population) were living with an income below the poverty line (less than USD 5.50 per day). Recent data suggest a sensible improvement, but the condition of rural areas continues to be far worse than the urban households: the proportion of people below the USD 1.90 line is up to four times higher in the countryside than in urban areas (Fiori, 2021). By the way, the rural working poor in Rio Grande is driven by the need for work, self-respect and dignity. It is not the case of extreme poverty as described in William Vollmann's *Poor People* (2007). There are, however, some exceptions.

Complementary Law No. 103 of July 14, 2000, authorized the Brazilian *estados* (states) and the Federal District to establish a minimum wage for employees not covered under a collective labor agreement (*convenção coletiva*) or company collective agreement (*acordo coletivo*): the minimum wage guarantees a threshold below which wages cannot fall. When hired on-the-books, no rural worker earns a wage below that which is established by the state government; in 2019, this was BRL 1236.15 a month for a 44-hour work week (approximately USD 220). When a local *convenção coletiva* exists, it brings the wage above this minimum, while other contractual clauses might even improve labor conditions, making rural workers' unions (i.e., the Sindicatos dos Trabalhadores Rurais, or STR) extremely important.

The second reason concerns the effects of the 2017 labor reform on working conditions and employer relations (Krein, 2018). Have these changes had an impact on labor relations? I mainly discuss two changes introduced by the reform: first, that now negotiated terms prevail over the law (meaning that the clauses of a collective agreement could either improve or even worsen labor conditions in relation to legal standards), and second, that the previously obligatory contribution of union dues out of one's paycheck became voluntary.

In Brazil, collective bargaining takes place at the local level rather than nationally. Each local trade union (*sindicato*) is responsible for collective bargaining in each municipality (*município*) or a region. Thus, there are 120 collective agreements in force in Rio Grande do Sul, covering 169 of the 497 municipalities of the state: of the approximately 400 rural workers' unions in the state, only 120 sign an agreement. Does the current system of representation adequately represent rural workers? Are there significant differences between rural workers' unions and, if so, why? What is a rural workers' union for? My interviews, the study of documentary sources and a data analysis try to answer these questions.

My approach is formally inductive: I am primarily interested in the life stories of rural workers (the so-called *assalariados*) as well as the symbolic universe within which they are embedded. Therefore, I conduct my analysis through a review of documentary sources, using comparison and abductive reasoning. The goal is to provide an overview of collective bargaining in Rio Grande do Sul and, where possible, to explain some specific aspects. I am interested both in working conditions (salary, workplace conditions, safety at work) and legal and social norms. I seek to explain labor conditions, therefore, in light of labor legislation and existing collective agreements.

According to the argument made by Peck (1996), labor markets develop in tandem with social and political institutions at the local or national level. It is important, therefore, to identify *where* the working poor exists: I mean the relationship among labor regulation, the rural socioeconomic environment (culture, values, meaning schemes) and the logic of collective action.

Theoretical Contributions

Within the state corporatism model of industrial relations, Brazilian unions are subordinate and subject to coercion by the state via numerous institutional mechanisms (Boito, 1991; Cook, 2007). This subordination also explains the lower level of social conflict: the *sindicato* is *pelego*—that is, a *sindicato* who is acting according to the interests of the employer rather than the workers'—because it is *incorporated* into the broader state apparatus. Unions are therefore incentivized to remain in this comfort zone, keeping conflict levels low and without introducing significant innovations in collective bargaining. However, some scholars have argued that the label *corporatist* does not adequately describe the Brazilian structure of unions. For instance, according to Noronha (2000), industrial relations are not based directly on the administrative state apparatus but rather on three "normative spaces" of labor relations: law, collective bargaining and company norms (defined unilaterally by the employer). The conclusions are not, however, particularly different from the state corporatism model: according to Noronha (2000), the action of unions is significantly curtailed—controlled by law with little room for collective action.

These theoretical contributions are relevant but limited. The approval of labor reform in 2017 raises some questions about the applicability of either a corporatist or legalistic framework. The normative space within which labor relations take place has been restructured, specifically by removing obligatory union dues and access to free representation within the labor courts. The law itself now establishes the supremacy of negotiated terms over labor law (Art. 620). Thus, if union funding has allowed control over trade unions, why should it be removed? My point of view is different: to some extent, both "legislative" and "corporatist" theories underestimate the efforts and achievements of labor unions as well as their ability to oppose anti-union policies (Carbonai, 2018). Some unions can be *pelegos*, but others, on the contrary, may be engaged on a daily basis, effectively representing the worker. Moreover, the history of a workers' union is not always linear but full of unexpected events over time (Ribeiro da Costa, 2019) and deserves increased attention around topics such as micro politics (Ortmann, 1995, p. 33), relations with political actors (Martins Rodrigues, 1990) and organizational structure and its paradoxes (Rodrigues & Ladosky, 2015).

I do not deny that the actors within organizations, and organizations as a whole, act under structural pressures, but these only limit the free choice of the actors. The 2017 labor reform intervenes in the trade unions' autonomy and functioning, weakening the entire trade union system (Colombi, 2019; Ganz, 2020). However, unions are always called upon to choose between a committed unionism or a *peleguismo sindacal*: for better or for worse, labor reform maintains this option for choice.

The local scenario is not very different from the national scenario. The reform has effects on the local system, but the local system also has room for action and options for choice. What is a rural union for? In Rio Grande do Sul, there are cases where, even if a *sindicato* exists, no collective bargaining takes place and there is no collective agreement signed. It is therefore important to study trade unions and union leaders, both committed and non-committed ones, and to understand the differences.

In the subject area of industrial relations, there are several impediments toward developing good theory (Müller-Jentsch, 2004). Existing theories are tailor-made for different institutions, actors and economic sectors due to the complexity of the subject area. A potential generally applicable theory put forward by Baccaro (2008) suggests that declining resources available to exert political influence forces unions to develop more inclusive and democratic procedures, where union members discuss and vote upon the decisions taken by union leaders. In this sense, there is a trade-off between contractual resources and democratic procedures: when resources are scarce, more investment is made in legitimization through democratic processes. Does this argument apply in the case of Brazil? Do internal democracy and rural workers' participation increase when there is a reduction in material incentives? The results of my research suggest that they do not.

According to industrial relations theory, when adopting a strategy for mobilization, unions generally seek to develop collective identity among their members so that, in the future, members are loyal, active and encourage other workers to take part in the union's struggles (Cregan et al., 2009). Does this argument also apply to rural workers in Rio Grande do Sul? When ethnographers study rural workers in Rio Grande do Sul closely, the *assalariados* appear reluctant to call strikes or express disagreement with their employers (Motta, 2019; Leal, 2021). This suggests that the societal and political culture necessary for collective action must be explored in further depth, with attention to details of the local context. In my findings, conflictual relations are quite latent if not completely absent.

Rural work and labor relations in the agricultural sector evade attempts to enclose them in a pre-established and adequate theory. Tasks such as picking tobacco leaves, watching over cattle and working on a rice plantation are not properly clean jobs. Hodson (1991, 2001) suggests that workers in "dirty jobs" utilize a series of mechanisms in order to remain satisfied with their jobs: (1) reconstructing (reframing) the meanings attributed to their tasks; (2) building spaces of autonomy within their work routine in which problem-solving skills can be expressed; (3) enhancing relationships with one or more fellow workers in a way that strengthens social relationships capable of building positive collective identities and developing mechanisms of solidarity within the group and (4) improving the set of tasks that these workers undertake on a daily basis. Is this framework appropriate to apply to rural workers? My findings suggest something slightly different—that these mechanisms are only partially activated.

Certainly, the existing debate surrounding trade union revitalization is important. Croucher and Wood (2017) suggest that the role of political activists is fundamental and must be considered. I therefore try to answer the following question: who are the political activists in Rio Grande do Sul who would currently be able to revitalize trade unions and resolve the precarious nature of rural work? Levesque and Murray (2006) argue that three sets of issues are fundamental for union revitalization: (1) enhancing basic union efficiency or instrumentality, (2) union governance and internal organization (3) and a rethinking of union resources. All three of these issues are explored and presented in my research findings.

The Brazilian rural labor movement has predominantly been studied from a historical point of view, which has included examining the historical role of social movements such as the Landless Rural Workers Movement (Movimento dos Sem Terra, or MST) and the rise of rural unionism (Maybury-Lewis, 1994; Bell, 1999; Coletti, 1998; Picolotto, 2014; Favareto, 2006). Additionally, there have been several studies about the health of rural workers in Rio Grande do Sul (Mendes & Werlang, 2014), especially with regard to the effect of pesticides on worker health (Viero et al., 2016; Ferreira de Siqueira et al., 2012). However, ethnographically oriented research is far less common, with some recent exceptions (Motta, 2019; Leal, 2021). Studies on the effects of the 2017 labor reform are even less present; for example, Gerhardt Lermen and Picolotto (2020) analyze the process of construction of labor rights of rural workers in Vacaria and evaluate the effects of the labor reform of 2017 on this process. They find out that the joint action of rural workers' unions, the Public Ministry of Labor and Labor Justice ensured a network of protection for rural workers while the labor reform of 2017 sought to weaken these institutions.

Methodological Notes

Interviews were conducted primarily in early 2020 and after June 2021. They took place either face to face or over the phone, following an unstructured approach. I visited 16 rural union's headquarters, taking pictures, collecting documents and observing the daily routine for hours.

A total of 55 interviews were conducted, including 21 union leaders, 15 rural salaried workers and 4 fazendeiros, along with other privileged

1 INTRODUCTION

witnesses. The union leaders were mainly presidents of rural workers' unions (STR). Respondents were chosen to represent different geographical regions of Rio Grande do Sul: the southern region (Sudeste Rio-Grandense), the so-called Campanha (Sudoueste Rio-grandense), the Porto Alegre metropolitan area (Metropolitana de Porto Alegre), the Serra (in the eastern part of the state, i.e., the Nordeste Rio-grandense), the Planalto (Noroeste Rio-grandense) and the central regions (Centro Ocidental and Centro Oriental Rio-grandense). I chose the entire state of Rio Grande do Sul because employers' and workers' union federations are

Fig. 1.1 Regions in Rio Grande do Sul

organized at the state level and the state government is a major player in crafting public policies for rural parts of the state (see Fig. 1.1).

After several failed attempts, I had to abandon my original plan to interview leaders of the landowners' unions (the *sindicatos ruralistas*). Ultimately, I obtained only one interview. However, I was still able to conduct interviews with some landowners (fazendeiros) who explained the organization of work on their fazendas.

The interviews vary in duration from twenty minutes to two hours. The interviews were generally conducted on the premises of the *sindicato*: the union leaders introduced me to their employees, showed me the union's premises and introduced me to rural workers who would come through the offices. When possible, I also visited some fazendas and two fruit packing companies.

My approach is inductive but certainly different from rural ethnographic studies such as those of Holmes (2013) and Horton (2016). These studies have a clear ethnographic bias while my research is more pragmatic. I especially preferred unstructured in-depth interviews: the questions are formed during the interview and the interviewees are free to say what they want. In fact, these interviews deal, in various cases, with very delicate issues. In addition to general questions, to ascertain rural unionism and labor conditions I introduced some situational questions to understand the interviewee's logic behind their action in a specific scenario: *In cases like that, what do you do? How did you handle [...]*? My purpose is also to take into consideration the practically adequate knowledge of each interviewee, more so than his or her opinions (Sayer, 1992, p. 70).

Most interviews were filmed; videos can be found on the following YouTube channel: https://www.youtube.com/user/davidecarbonai/. Interviews are identified with the tag "rural workers". Other interviews in audio format can be found on the following podcast: https://open.spotify.com/show/14Fqtgd2vP8y9PrHhyOcmA (Carbonai & Lentz, 2020). The purpose of this is to make research materials publicly available. The concept of public ethnography, as discussed by Vannini (2019), is to make available the various research materials used in the course of the study, such as filmed interviews or unstructured interview recordings.

I also try to preserve the anonymity of the interviewees. I use the following identifiers in ordinary cases; for example: [STR 1, Santana do Livramento] means that the interviewee is the first of two local union leaders at the workers' union (STR) of Santana do Livramento. Sometimes, I prefer to completely hide the identity of the interviewee; in this case I use the following wording: [STR, XXX].

The research follows an approach informed by inductive methods (Pickens & Braun, 2018). Interview transcripts are closely examined to identify common themes, topics, ideas and patterns of meaning. The recurring themes reported by rural workers are subsequently analyzed and explored comparatively between interviewees. Generally speaking, the coding that is used and the themes that are developed are directed by the content of the data. The focus, however, is maintained on the relationships between rural works, *sindicatos*, and collective bargaining.

The data in Chap. 3 are extracted from the Brazilian government's CAGED system (https://bi.mte.gov.br/bgcaged/). The data on *convenções* are extracted from the federal system of collective bargaining, Mediador: http://www3.mte.gov.br/sistemas/mediador. Regional geographical classifications follow those used by the FEE (https://arquivofee.rs.gov.br/). Also, trade union federations provided data about the presence of unions in the *municípios* of Rio Grande do Sul. I explore these data and conduct a multiple correspondence analysis (Di Franco, 2006). This study is primarily qualitative, but this quantitative analysis reinforces the findings from the qualitative interviews.

This study offers new insights into the relationship between rural working poverty, collective bargaining and rural unions. In some cases, collective bargaining cannot significantly improve working conditions. It is, therefore, important to consider the structure of collective bargaining, union efforts and the latent conflict present in rural employment relations. What contractual clauses settled through collective bargaining safeguard the rights and health of rural workers? What has changed since the labor reform was enacted?

The final arguments follow an abductive logic. According to Randal Collins (1985, p. 188), abduction is a mode of inference by which one moves from one set of ideas to a conclusion in another set of ideas. To improve salary and labor conditions, collective bargaining at the local level is of extreme importance. Moreover, before the 2017 labor reform, the *imposto sindical* allowed workers' unions, at least, to pay the health care costs of rural workers and their families. The fragmentation of union representation in too many individual unions is another important emerging theme. The workers therefore fail to understand the logic of collective action: protests and strikes are practically absent. The result of this is a generally unstable framework which favors the strongest party in labor relations.

The differences between the agrarian systems of Rio Grande do Sul are due to profound historical reasons which I do not pretend to discuss here (Silva Neto & Basso, 2015). However, it is worth mentioning the historical distinction between the Colonial North—whose cultural matrix is that of European immigrants, especially Germans and Italians who arrived in the nineteenth century—with little slavery and the predominance of family farming, and the South, with an Iberian matrix, the predominance of large estates and the extensive use of slave labor. Bandeira (2003) points out that the endowment of social capital is significantly higher in the Colonial North than in the South: a multitude of recreational associations, social clubs, and an intense collaborative and cooperative social life among the first settlers are present in the Colonial North, while community life is more fragile in the South. These contrasts are mirrored in the political and economic system of Rio Grande do Sul (Baquero & Prá, 2007), but the different endowments of social capital don't guarantee more inclusive labor relations or a better quality of work for rural wage earners.

Plan of the Book

In the introduction I discuss the main theoretical contributions and my methodology. I also present the logic of my arguments. In Chap. 2, I introduce a selection of interviews with rural workers and explore class identity along with issues related to work safety. I also introduce the trade union culture and the relationship between workers and fazendeiros. In Chap. 3, I present the trade union structure and how collective bargaining takes place in the rural sector. In Chap. 4, I bring together concepts previously introduced and discuss the problems of labor representation and regulation. In the conclusion, I discuss ways of overcoming the current impasse of rural trade unionism.

References

Baccaro, L. (2008). Contrattazione politica e consultazione dei lavoratori. *Quaderni di Rassegna sindacale, 9*(1), 125–135.
Bandeira, P. S. (2003). Algumas Hipóteses sobre as Causas das Diferenças Regionais quanto ao Capital Social no Rio Grande do Sul. In S. M. Correa de Souza (Ed.), *Capital Social e Desenvolvimento Regional*. Edunisc.

Baquero, M., & Prá, J. R. (2007). *A democracia brasileira e a cultura política no Rio Grande do Sul*. UFRGS Editora.

Bell, S. (1999). *Campanha Gaúcha: A Brazilian ranching system, 1850–1920*. Stanford University Press.

Boito, A. (1991). *O sindicalismo de Estado no Brasil: uma análise crítica da estrutura sindical*. Editora da Unicamp.

Carbonai, D. (2018). Labour reform in Brazil, politics, and sindicatos: Notes on the general strikes of 2017. *Journal of Politics in Latin America, 11*(2), 231–245. https://doi.org/10.1177/1866802X19861493

Carbonai, D., & Lentz J. R. L. (Host). (2020). *Sociologia do trabalho*. https://open.spotify.com/show/14Fqtgd2vP8y9PrHhyOcmA

Coletti, C. (1998). *A estrutura sindical no campo*. Unicamp.

Collins, R. (1985). *Three sociological traditions*. Oxford University.

Colombi, A. P. (2019). As Centrais Sindicais e a Reforma Trabalhista. Enfrentamentos e Dificuldades. *Tempo Social, 31*(3), 217–236. https://doi.org/10.11606/0103-2070.ts.2019.152129

Cook, M. L. (2007). *The politics of labour reform in Latin America: between flexibility and rights*. The Pennsylvania State University.

Cregan, C., Bartram, T., & Stanton, P. (2009). Union organizing as a mobilizing strategy: The impact of social identity and transformational leadership on the collectivism of union members. *British Journal of Industrial Relations, 47*(4), 701–722.

Croucher, R., & Wood, G. (2017). Union renewal in historical perspective. *Work, Employment and Society, 31*(6), 1010–1020. https://doi.org/10.1177/0950017017713950

Di Franco, G. (2006). *Corrispondenze multiple e altre tecniche multivariate per variabili categoriali*. Milan, Franco Angeli.

Favareto, A. (2006). Agricultores, Trabalhadores: os Trinta Anos do Novo Sindicalismo Rural no Brasil. *Revista Brasileira de Ciências Sociais, 21*(62), 27–44. https://doi.org/10.1590/S0102-69092006000300002

Ferreira de Siqueira, D., De Moura, R. M., Laurentino, G. C., Silva, G. F., Soares, L. D., & Lima, B. R. (2012). Qualidade de Vida de Trabalhadores Rurais e Agrotóxicos: uma Revisão Sistemática. *Revista Brasileira de Ciências da Saúde, 16*(2), 259–266. https://doi.org/10.4034/RBCS.2012.16.02.22

Fiori, T. (2021). *Erradicação da pobreza: ODS 1 no Rio Grande do Sul*. Secretaria de Planejamento.

Ganz, L. C. (2020). A reforma das relações sindicais volta ao debate no Brasil. *Estudos Avançados, 34*(98), 127–142. https://doi.org/10.1590/s0103-4014.2020.3498.009

Gerhardt Lermen, N., & Picolotto, L. E. (2020). Trabalho rural, representação classista e lutas por direitos na produção de maçãs em Vacaria. *Revista Da ABET, 19*(1). https://doi.org/10.22478/ufpb.1676-4439.2020v19n1.52355

Hodson, R. (1991). The active worker: Compliance and autonomy at the workplace. *Journal of Contemporary Ethnography, 20*, 47–78.

Hodson, R. (2001). *Dignity at work.* Cambridge University Press.

Holmes, S. (2013). *Fresh fruit, broken bodies: Migrant farmworkers in the United States.* University of California Press, ProQuest Ebook Central.

Horton, S. B. (2016). *They leave their kidneys in the fields: Illness, injury, and illegality among U.S. farmworkers.* University of California Press.

Krein, J. D. (2018). O desmonte dos direitos, as novas configurações do trabalho e o esvaziamento da ação coletiva: consequências da reforma trabalhista. *Tempo Social, 30*(1), 77–104. https://doi.org/10.11606/0103-2070.ts.2018.138082

Leal, O. F. (2021). *Os gaúchos: cultura e identidade masculina no pampa.* Tomo Editorial.

Levesque, C., & Murray, G. (2006). How do unions renew? Paths to union renewal. *Labour Studies Journal, 31*(3), 1–13. https://doi.org/10.1177/0160449X0603100301

Martins Rodrigues, L. (1990). *Partidos e Sindicatos.* Ática.

Maybury-Lewis, B. (1994). *The politics of the possible: The Brazilian rural workers' trade union movement, 1964–1985.* Temple University Press.

Mendes, R. J. M., & Werlang, R. (2014). Suicídio no Meio rural no Rio Grande do Sul. In Á. R. Crespo, C. G. Bottega, & K. V. Perez (Eds.), *Atenção à saúde mental do trabalhador: sofrimento e transtornos psíquicos relacionados ao trabalho.* Evangraf.

Motta, G. (2019). Trabalho Assalariado e Trabalhadores Indígenas nos Pomares de Maçã no Sul do Brasil. *Unpublished doctoral dissertation.* Instituto de Filosofia e Ciências Sociais, Universidade Federal do Rio de Janeiro.

Müller-Jentsch, W. (2004). Theoretical approaches to industrial relations. In B. Kaufmann (Ed.), *Theoretical perspectives on work and the employment relationship.* IRRA Series.

Noronha, E. G. (2000). O modelo legislado de relações de trabalho no Brasil. *Dados, 43*(2). https://doi.org/10.1590/S0011-52582000000200002

Ortmann, G. (1995). *Formen der Produktion: Organisation und Rekursivität.* Westdeutscher Verlag.

Peck, J. (1996). *Work-place: The social regulation of labour markets.* The Guilford Press.

Pickens, C., & Braun, V. (2018). 'Stroppy bitches who just need to learn how to settle'? Young single women and norms of femininity and heterosexuality. *Sex Roles, 79*(7–8), 431–448. https://doi.org/10.1177/0891243209340034

Picolotto, E. L. (2014). A formação de um sindicalismo de agricultores familiares no Sul do Brasil. *Sociologias, 16*(35), 204–236. https://doi.org/10.1590/S15174522014000100008

Ribeiro da Costa, L. A. (2019). A estrutura sindical e a negociação coletiva brasileira nos anos 2000 e os primeiros impactos da Reforma Trabalhista (Lei 13.467/17). *XVI Encontro nacional ABET.* Salvador (BA).

Rodrigues, I. J., & Ladosky, M. H. G. (2015). Paradoxos do sindicalismo brasileiro: a CUT e os trabalhadores rurais. *Lua Nova: Revista de Cultura e Política, 95*, 87–142. https://doi.org/10.1590/0102-6445087-142/95

Sayer, R. A. (1992). *Method in social science: A realist approach.* Psychology Press.

Silva Neto, B., & Basso D. (2015). *Os sistemas agrários do Rio Grande do Sul: análise e recomendações de políticas.* Ijui, Editora Unijuí.

Vannini, P. (2019). *Doing public ethnography. How to create and disseminate ethnographic and qualitative research to wide audiences.* Routledge.

Viero, C. M., Camponogara, S., Cezar-Vaz, M. R., da Costa, V. Z., & Beck, C. L. (2016). Sociedade de risco: o uso dos agrotóxicos e implicações na saúde do trabalhador rural. *Escola Anna Nery, 20*(1), 99–105. https://doi.org/10.5935/1414-8145.20160014

Vollmann, W. T. (2007). *Poor people.* Ecco.

CHAPTER 2

Rural Salaried Workers

Abstract This chapter discusses class identity, working conditions and precarious conditions in the labor market. It also analyses the identity and material constraints of rural workers.

Keywords Class identity • Safety at work • Slave labor

Frantz and Silva Neto (2015) have listed the predominant regional systems of agricultural production in Rio Grande do Sul. Soybeans are planted throughout the northern regions, rice is cultivated near the western border with Argentina and Uruguay and the use of machinery for large-scale harvesting takes place in the west and north regions. The largest farms (estâncias and fazendas) are present above all in the extensive plains of the Campanha and the South (i.e., the Pampa), whereas farms are smaller in the Serra and the Planalto to the east, on the border with the Brazilian state of Santa Catarina. Tasks vary according to regional differences, methods of cultivation and agricultural production: there is a higher number of permanent employees in the Pampa and the regions around Vacaria (where I also found very active rural workers' unions) and a larger presence of skilled workers in the western and northern regions. However,

© The Author(s), under exclusive license to Springer Nature
Switzerland AG 2022
D. Carbonai, *Rural Workers, Sindicatos and Collective Bargaining in Rio Grande do Sul*, https://doi.org/10.1007/978-3-030-94808-5_2

these regional differences disappear in relation to political participation: protests and strikes are absent almost everywhere.

It is worth mentioning that the prevailing historiography of rural workers in Rio Grande do Sul identifies some typical elements of the gaucho's identity. Gauchos have been portrayed as rural wage laborers, living in the plains and hills of the Pampa, skilled in farming, herding cattle, horses and sheep, and as excellent horsemen. Scholars identify a tension between nature and culture: the need for the aerial life, a thousand elements of the physical and moral life of the gaucho take shape from his skeleton to the most tender expansion of his feelings, where the habitus incorporates the dimension of the countryside as well as traditional food and music (Leal, 2021). The interviews conducted as part of the research presented in this book, on the other hand, point out significant differences. In a certain sense, the melancholic loneliness of the gaucho transforms into complacency, and even resignation. Also, agricultural production systems have changed over time, impacting the number of *assalariados*, tasks and workplace conditions (Frantz & Silva Neto, 2015). Even the landscape of the Pampa itself has changed under the weight of livestock grazing, and the expansion of pine and eucalyptus farming has paralleled these changes (Oliveira, 2020). This romanticized relationship between man and nature has evolved over time and has become less idealized.

Nowadays, finding typical elements of identity among rural workers has become much rarer. By the way, the rural workers I interviewed do not even mention the term "class" or the expression "working class". On the contrary, instead of "work", interviewees prefer to use the term "service" (i.e., the *serviço, prestar serviço*). However, while "work" produces "workers", "service" produces "servants".

Class Identity

My methodology contrasts with the hypothetic-deductive approach and involves the application of inductive reasoning. Usually, a study based in grounded theory (Strauss & Corbin, 1998) is likely to begin with a question or with the collection of qualitative data. I begin my first interviews with rural salaried workers by asking these questions: *What time do you get up in the morning? How is your working day?*

> I get up at 6 o'clock. At 6:50 I take the bus. We start working from 7.40, until noon. Then we work until 17.30. I have to work, right. I am a tractor

driver. [...] Apple picking is even more tiring. My salary is BRL 1584 [in 2021], a little higher than the others. The others get around of BRL 1300. The work is also dangerous [...] I don't talk to anyone when I'm working. (Rural worker 1, Vacaria)

I get up at 6 o'clock. I ride a horse to work every day. It takes me an hour. [...] We must thank God for having a job. (Rural worker, Mostardas)

You get up when the sun comes up. And you work the whole day. (Rural worker, Alegrete)

I get up at five. I harvest tobacco leaves. I am a day laborer. I earn BRL 100 a day [...] The employer doesn't sign my labor book [*carteira de trabalho*]. (Rural worker, Venáncio Aires)

I get up early in the morning, at 6:30. Very early. I take a bus to work. I work the day shift. My husband works the night shift. At least I see him at lunch. One stays at home to take care of the kids. I go home when I finish my shift and take care of the children. (Rural worker 4, Vacaria)

I live here [on the farm]. The owner pays me to live here and look after the cattle. I get up early in the morning, but during the night I check if everything is fine [...] He pays me a little more than the minimum wage. (Rural worker, São Borja)

I get up early in the morning. Here, we work. They pay. It is a decent job. They treat me with respect. (Rural worker 3, Vacaria)

Rural workers appreciate their job. It is considered tiring and poorly paid but "it is a service" and everybody needs a job: "you have to work to raise your family and pay the bills [...] and thank God we have a job" (Rural worker 6, Vacaria).

Fernanda tells me about her work on a fazenda near Arroio Grande (in the southern region of Rio Grande do Sul). She is currently retired, and she misses her job.

This is my story. I grew up in the countryside, with my family, like others in the area. In Arroio Grande, or really, 70 kilometers outside of the town, in the countryside. Then, I worked and lived with my husband. I needed a job. There was a rice plantation. Now it's soy. We worked with everything: cattle, sheep [...] I used to live there. I got up at 7 am and I worked until noon. I took care of the horses [...] then I sold the cattle [...] There was a *capataz* [foreman], but I had a good relationship with the *patrão* [the employer] and I worked directly with him. The work is tiring. Those who come from the countryside can say that it is even pleasant. You are in contact with nature. It was my life. I lived there with my husband. Life is pretty tough, especially during the harvest. There is a deadline for planting. It's pretty tiring but it's an interesting life. [...] In our region there is not much exploitation. When they [the farmers] comply with our collective agreement, there is no slave labor. [...] If the law is enforced, then there is no exploitation. (Rural worker, Arroio Grande)

Antônio was a *capataz* [foreman]: he managed other rural workers on a large fazenda in Alegrete (on the western border of Rio Grande do Sul). He is retired but continues working. Antônio recalls the gauchos of 30 years ago, as described by Ondina Leal (2021). He tells me about his working day, when they founded the local *sindicato* ("more than thirty years ago") and the trusting relationship he had with his *patrão* (i.e., the fazendeiro). His family lived on the outskirts of Alegrete, but he lived on the farm (like Fernanda and many others rural workers, especially on the large plots of land in the Pampa). He was always respected by his *patrão*:

I got up at five o'clock. Until noon, I took care of horses, cattle. I had rodeos. [...] All by the rules. The *patrão* paid for everything. I started working when I was 12 years old. I had a fight with another student at school, so I decided to leave town and go to work on the farm. And with God's help I kept working, until today [...] He is a good *patrão* [the current one] There are good *patrões* and bad ones. The old *patrões* were better. Their heirs are much worse. They are nastier They inherited their father's land. And then working conditions got worse. In the place where once there were five *peões*, they put two. In the place of two, they put only one. [...] It is not possible to support a family with a salary of BLR 1200. Now, if the *patrão* doesn't pay me a little more, I won't even show up to work. I have a small car now. [...] Today, at 75 years old, I dance and make love. And I continue to work with a salary much higher than the minimum, and I negotiate the conditions of my job. Now I just want to work on a smaller property. (Rural worker, Alegrete)

He mentions that on the big ranches where he worked, there was an overseer, a cook and several *peões* (unskilled and semi-skilled rural agricultural workers). His schedule was defined by the daily routines of livestock

2 RURAL SALARIED WORKERS

farming. When he was no longer satisfied with his *patrão*, he stopped working and looked for another employer.

Talking with rural workers and union leaders, I realized that some parts of this cultural heritage can still be observed today, but that the common identity belonging to gauchos has mostly faded away. Interviewees also interpret the gaucho identity in a different way. One interviewee was quite clear:

> That world no longer exists. No. All of that no longer exists. The gaucho on horseback? Drinking chimarrão? Today, they are employees who managed to buy a car. Always paying in installments. That mythical person no longer exists. (Sindicato de Trabalhadores Rurais [STR], Arroio Grande)

Rural workers at the fazendas are also isolated: "they work in the middle of the fields" (STR, Alegrete). This physical distance is not trivial: "it is difficult to meet, participate in meetings, discuss among ourselves" (STR, Uruguaiana).

Roberto is the president of the Dona Quitéria Quilombola Community Association in Mostardas (a municipality in the southern region of Rio Grande do Sul). The *quilombo* was a place of refuge for enslaved Africans who escaped from the fazenda or for outlaws of African descent. Roberto identifies not with gaucho music and poetry but with his African roots, "the suffering of my people", the *quilombola* community and God. He also looks to maintain a dignified standard of living: a small house, albeit isolated in the rural outskirts of Mostardas. Like many other rural wage earners, Roberto cultivates his own small farm next to his house which, although it is small, allows him to sell sweet potatoes and other vegetables.

> Our association has a group of rural workers. The association is an organization within the *quilombola* community. We take care of livestock. Sheep. We also plant for food, sweet potatoes, corn. I worked 32 years with a formal contract. The work is tiring. It goes on day after day. I went eight kilometers, every day, riding a horse. I leave home early in the morning. [...] I'm the foreman. I coordinate the work. I've been a foreman for 6 years. Before, I worked as a simple salaried worker [*peão*]. Today, the boss is calm. He rarely shows up. Only once in a while. [...] There is high unemployment in this region. The association tries to help other community members. We have a president and a vice president. We also deal with issues of the work itself. But it is more at work that we deal with wage issues. Our boss respects the *convenção*. He pays above the *convenção*. There are colleagues of mine

> who earn more, others who earn less. In the region, in general, a worker earns little: BRL 1300, more or less. But I want to work here, on that farm. It is better. [...] We are always looking for a new job. We must work. If we find a good *patrão*, we stay longer. Otherwise, we look for another one who pays better. [...] In our community we have young people working in the countryside. There are also young agronomists who studied at the university. Yes, young people from the quilombo who have studied. The community has evolved. [...] We have suffered a lot. Our enslaved ancestors suffered. Today we are free. And getting help. The Bolsonaro government is not helping us, but the previous ones did. [...] I tell others in the community that BLR 1300 is not much, but better times will come. (Rural worker, Mostardas)

When Roberto talks about the children of the *quilombolas* who went to university, he says that "they have a profession". There is a "profession" and there are rural jobs (i.e., a "service"): a salary of BRL 1300 per month, which "isn't enough to rent an apartment or house in the urban center of Mostardas but you can live decently, and things can get better with a service" (rural worker, Mostardas). Rural workers living at the *quilombo* strengthen their identity relations: they represent one of the few groups capable of building positive collective identities—although these identities are defined on the basis of the redemption of African slaves deported to Brazil—and developing mechanisms of solidarity within the group (Hodson, 2001).

I spent a whole day with Bruno, in Venâncio Aires, a municipality in the tobacco plantation region. Bruno showed me how the tobacco leaves are harvested and how the drying process works.

> Here the majority of people work without a signed *carteira de trabalho* [labor book]. We are day laborers [...] I am fine. I would like to have a field of my own to plant tobacco, but family farmers have to fill out a lot of paperwork. I don't know, maybe I prefer to work as an *assalariado*. (Rural worker, Venâncio Aires)

It is not easy to discuss wage and labor issues with rural workers: they do not want to reveal tense workplace relations, mention the possibility of a strike or talk about collective mobilization; on the one hand, they are satisfied, but on the other hand, they complain about low wages and working conditions. Unions leaders and rural workers themselves often use the term *tímido* (i.e., shy) to describe the *assalariados*. This shyness comes across in interviews, perhaps because "the *assalariado* is always intimidated by the *patrão*" (STR, Venâncio Aires).

> Rural workers are shy. I see it, here, in my community. (Rural worker, Mostardas)

> 'Don't go to the union. You don't need it!' The *patrão* says. (STR, Uruguaiana)

> The *patrão* tries to do everything to avoid the worker contacting the union. (Contar, Brasília)

> You don't see the *assalariados* here at the union premises. We also have a collective agreement. They should come and become a member of the union. They could use our services as well. Every year, we hold an assembly to approve the collective agreement, but nobody shows up. Workers comes to the union to see how much they will receive as severance pay [...] most of them don't even appear. It's hard to get... it's complicated. We know that we have 300 rural workers here. Where are they? In any case, the *assalariado* is always intimidated by the *patrão*. It is the *patrão* who commands. (STR, Venâncio Aires)

The relationship between rural workers and their union is often limited to the medical assistance services that several *sindicatos* provide. My data may not involve a large sample, but interviewees are unique: "with few exceptions, workers do not even know if there is a signed collective agreement in force or not" (STR, Santa Cruz do Sul). If I ask a regular hired *assalariado* who frequently uses the local *sindicato*'s services (if the union in question makes them available), it is likely that he knows of the presence of a collective agreement. However, when I meet a worker who does not have a formal job and who works and lives in a rural area, it is likely that he knows little to nothing about bargaining, trade unions or labor rights.

> They don't even have a clue about the existence of a collective agreement. (STR, Venâncio Aires)

> Is there a union in town? Yes. But is it for the employees or only for small farmers? [...] My colleagues don't know anything about it. [...] I know there is a collective agreement, but many *assalariados* don't. (Rural worker, Venâncio Aires)

> Here, there are many *assalariados*. There are also many *caseiros* [a rural worker who lives in the fazenda, generally alone, and takes care of the house and the cattle]. Sometimes employees have been formally hired with a labor book [*carteira de trabalho*], sometimes not. There are the good *assalariados* and the bad ones. There are drunks. [...] They don't know anything about unions or collective agreements. They don't know what these things are. (Fazendeiro, São Borja)

> Once there was a rural worker who was wearing a Farsul t-shirt. Yes, the employers' union. And he was proud of it. He failed to understand the difference among workers' and employers' unions. (STR, Arroio Grande)

When the union is active, it offers medical services, and union leaders reach out to rural workers: "you find workers who appreciate the *sindicato* and know what a collective agreement is" (STR 2, Vacaria). On the contrary, when the union for some reason is not interested in representing workers (which is in several cases as I will soon explain) and doesn't make itself relevant to them, the *assalariados* are completely isolated and know nothing about the *sindicato*, social assistance service for workers or labor rights. It is therefore difficult to build a class identity. Thus, other identities, albeit blurred and incongruent, take over: "keeping the family", "thinking for oneself", "God", "to be a good man", "the service", "the right way", "hold on and carry on".

In a focus group with three female workers in Vacaria, I was trying to understand *how* they discussed work and wages as well as their relationship with the union. I was curious to see *how* they argued trade union issues among themselves. One worker suggested that trade union issues are associated with politics, which often causes embarrassment. In times of crisis, especially when working for a large fruit packing company such as the one in Vacaria, it is better to avoid talking about politics at work and settle for what you already have:

> I thank God for being here, for having my job. Sure, it could be better, but it could also be much worse. [...] We are fine. We work. They treat us well. We can't complain. [...] There is no talk of politics at work. It is better for us. (Rural worker 7, Vacaria)

Following up, I asked the worker if one can live decently with a salary like hers.

> We have many problems. Gas, electricity, rent. I have a lot of expenses. Luckily my daughter is grown up and she is working right now. It's hard. (Rural worker 7, Vacaria)

There is not much room to develop class identity. Some *assalariados* have a backyard garden (some even have a larger field where they can raise some cattle), and they hope to become small farmers one day. A rural worker in Vacaria told me the following:

> My husband owns a small plot of land. If I had better conditions, I would even change jobs. My husband lives on the farm. I was born on that farm. We have some animals there, but there are no conditions to make a living from it. We have few animals. I can't stop working now. Who knows, maybe one day I will raise cattle. (Rural worker 5, Vacaria)

Building a class identity is also difficult because of the physical distance between fazendas (and among workers) as well as because of the political and social climate.

> The farms are far from each other. Several fazendas have no easy access to the road. The worker is isolated during the work shift and the fazendeiros don't let trade unionists in. Workers don't talk about politics... and they don't talk about politics also because the *patrão* is in any case fan of Bolsonaro [...] while unions are 'the absolute evil'. (STR, XX)

> These days, it's best not to discuss politics at work. You cannot predict the reactions of the employer. And my colleagues are all a little afraid to discuss politics. (Rural worker 3, Vacaria)

The word "class" appeared just two times in my interviews, and it was not a rural salaried worker who mentioned the term. The first time it was the president of a local *sindicato ruralista* (i.e., fazendeiros' union).

> The *sindicato* [*ruralista*] must defend our class interests, those of the farmers, be they small or large. There are no differences between farmers. (*Sindicato ruralista*, Arroio Grande)

The second time, it was in an interview with the president of a local STR in Caxias do Sul:

Since December of last year [2020], we no longer represent the *assalariados*, just family farmers [...] We have never signed a specific collective agreement for the *assalariados*. The *assalariados* are another class. They are not family farmers. They should unionize, in a different class than ours. (STR, Caxias do Sul)

The mention of class in the first interview did not particularly surprise me, nor did the fact that it was mentioned by a representative of the fazendeiros who defined the fazendeiros as a single social class. This second interview, however, intrigues me. It is assumed that the president of a local STR represents rural workers, but that's not quite the case. Why did an STR leader tell me that the *assalariados* belong to another class?

Safety at Work

Rural work is not only poorly paid but also very risky. In Rio Grande do Sul, the official number of fatal workplace accidents in agriculture is significant and has risen from 59 in 2018 to 77 as of November 2019 (Fetar, 2019). The cause is mainly accidents involving tractors (19 in 2018, 23 in 2019) or electric shock (12 in 2018, 9 in 2019). However, accidents that happen to informal workers are not recorded in police reports. Scholars point out a significant difference between officially registered accidents measured by workers' compensation claims (139 deaths in 2016, across all economic sectors) and the official records obtained from the police and public health authorities (Rodrigues et al., 2019), who registered at least 506 victims of fatal occupational accidents in 2016, 502 of which were due to violent causes. The survey also reports that the highest fatal accident rates involve small businesses, unregistered workers and the agricultural, civil construction and cargo transportation sectors. Considering this, the number of fatal accidents in the agricultural sector could exceed 200 victims per year in Rio Grande do Sul, out of a total of about 160,000 workers, including both formally hired and informal workers (Fetar, 2019).

A 2001 survey has signaled the risks of the workplace in rural Rio Grande do Sul (Fehlberg et al., 2001). Out of the 580 respondents, 63 rural workers (11%) reported at least one work-related accident in the previous 12 months. There were 82 accidents during the study period, mainly related to the use of hand farm tools (29%) and livestock management (27%). The main types of injuries were cuts (50%), bruises (13%) and burns (9%). The body areas most frequently involved were hands (34%), feet (29%) and legs (18%). Among the injured rural workers, only 32% were treated for their wounds or injuries.

Interviewees reported the circumstances of accidents in detail, as well as the union's support and the often-questionable attitudes of the fazendeiros. One example comes from an interview with Juvenal (a rural salaried worker living in Uruguaiana, a municipality located at the western end of the state of Rio Grande do Sul) and Olíbio (the president of the Uruguaiana rural workers' union). I met them in a neighborhood on the outskirts of Uruguaiana. Juvenal suffered a serious work accident a few weeks before the interview: the incident led to the amputation of three fingers on his left hand. Juvenal explained the work accident:

> I was taking care of the harvest. The *patrão* put a kid to work on the machine, a thresher, but he wasn't very prepared. I wanted him to put someone on it who understood it better, but he said: 'No, I'll put my cousin on it, because the kid is the one who will do the cutting' [...] And the kid kept the machine cutting, but the machine got clogged. I went to assist the boy. I had a look, I cleaned out what was stuck inside and I went to the other side of the tractor, and when I pulled a strap, the kid pressed a button in the cabin and my hand went down [...]. They didn't call an ambulance. There was a trucker there [...] He took me to town. And from there, directly to the UPA [emergency care unit]. I was brought to Santa Casa Hospital and there [...] I had surgery, and everything. Then, when everything passed, I spoke to Olíbio [the local STR leader] and he took me to the police station to register the incident, the work accident. The *patrão* did not even show up to the hospital, from April until now [...] nothing. We went to court; we made a deal, and everything passed. He paid nothing. After that, I reported [the accident] to the local police [...] Now, he must give me 600 bags of rice a year and pay the equivalent of 48 months of minimum wage over 4 years. That was the deal, but I don't know if I'll get it, right [...] 600 bags per year for 4 harvests, every April 30th, he must give them to me. (Rural worker 1, Uruguaiana)

In other cases, the *sindicato* intervened only after the accident, when it did at all. Some unions carried out work safety campaigns, especially those affiliated with Fetar. However, not all workers' unions are committed to work safety issues.

In Uruguaiana, I also met other rural salaried workers. Euclides told me of when he had a kidney stone and the *patrão* took advantage of the illness to fire him.

> It happened in May 2019. I was harvesting [...] and I suddenly felt sick. I was eating and it hurt [...]. They brought me into town. They took me to the emergency room where they ran some tests, and they found a kidney stone. I was treating myself on my own [...]; I requested worker's compensation, but they told me that they didn't have any money [...] and they said to me, 'if you want, I'll make a deal with you'. I said 'ok' at the time [...] I didn't know anything. I didn't expect that I would be without unemployment insurance. The owner did not want to report the issue to the *sindicato*, but I did. The boss told me that they had no relationship with the *sindicato* [...]. I worked on everything, with grease, oil, did everything [...]. I was working at this company for 18 years. In June, I turn 60. (Rural worker 2, Uruguaiana)

Euclides underwent surgery. The local *sindicato* collected the necessary documentation to receive disability from the INSS (Instituto Nacional do Seguro Social) [National Institute of Social Security] and attempted to make a deal with the company so that they could forward the necessary documentation for Euclides to receive unemployment insurance.

> This is the effect of the lack of supervision and accountability on the part of the ministry and public authorities. There are workers who haven't been able to take a vacation for two years. Fazendeiros don't pay overtime. Sometimes, we can make things a little better, sometimes not: it depends on the worker's education level too. Sometimes workers only learn how to read and then begin working, dropping out of school [...] if we didn't act, he [Euclides] would be out of the INSS, unprotected and perhaps using his savings to support his family. The labor reform affected the social security system. One affected the other [...] Think about the countryside, where a worker may be 70 km away from his workplace and where the public transport system is precarious. A working day is just enough to pay the bus fare, and if the salary isn't enough to earn minimum wage for the month, then you must add from your own pocket to be able to count on social security benefits. This labor reform has hit the rural worker hard. (STR, Uruguaiana)

Multiple causes and conditions determine working conditions and workplace safety. One of the questions raised by the interviewees is the so-called *polivalência legal* [legal polyvalence]: the multitasking rural worker.

> Because of *polivalência*, a rural worker can be required to perform various tasks (land preparation, planting, cultural treatment, harvesting, cleaning,

etc.), handling different equipment. Our *sindicato* suggests that we avoid multitasking. The rural worker can't do everything [...] the rural worker is not an electrician [...] and the *sindicato* advises rural workers not to do dangerous tasks or operate machines without experience. What then happens in practice... (STR, Alegrete)

The risks are generally unexpected. It is recognized that working in the fields is dangerous, but prevention measures are not always planned.

Two days ago, by mistake, a worker used a sheep tick lotion in the cattle bath, which resulted in the death of the animals. The worker was also taken to the hospital. The worker knew nothing about using that substance. All this, unfortunately, is ordinary. (STR, Alegrete)

A health and safety inspector from the Ministry of Economic Affairs commented on a fatal work accident that took place in Cruz Alta a few weeks before the interview:

A rural employee was driving a dump truck when a problem occurred with the rear bucket. The worker stopped the truck, got out and went to check the problem in the back; then the bucket fell on the worker, who died instantly. (Ministério Público do Trabalho [MPT] 1, Porto Alegre)

Workers involved in maintenance operations must, by law, be trained for the safety of their work activities. In the inspector's technical report about the accident in Cruz Alta (in addition to non-compliance with certain technical standards) it was found that the workers were not trained to perform ordinary working procedures. Additionally, the rural worker was alone at the time of the incident, which occurred in an isolated place: "unfortunately, his workmates arrived late to the scene of the accident" (MPT 1, Porto Alegre).

Respondents report serious problems regarding job security that have increased with the closure of the Ministry of Labor (as determined by Bolsonaro's government) and the end of free access to labor courts (which is no longer guaranteed since the approval of the 2017 labor reform). Because of the labor reform, inspections on the farms are reduced, it is more difficult to reach out to the workers and the support of the public inspectors is no longer easily available. With regard to these issues, interviewees are univocal and unambiguous:

> The labor reform has had a great impact. The field is not a factory. It is not the same. You can't go with a loudspeaker to the entrance to the farm and call all the workers, like in the metallurgical sector. You must visit the fazendas, going from farm to farm. But they have their doors closed, whether for safety reasons or to inhibit the union or the Ministry of Labor. The fazendeiro says: 'they visit the *fazenda* to meddle'. In the *convenção* [collective agreement], there is even a clause, under which the union has the possibility to visit the farm, but the farmer doesn't allow this [...] Also, today, the inspectors of the labor ministry do not have the financial means to visit and control the fazendas. They don't have money for gasoline and do not receive per diems to travel overnight. (Contar, Brasília)

> After 2017, inspections decreased. They opened space for the fazendeiros. In large companies, everything is fine, but in the countryside inspections decreased. Informality increased. Oversight decreased even in large companies [...]. You have 30% fewer labor lawsuits. If the worker loses, he must pay the court fees. The courts are booked from today until May of next year. [...] The government's intention is to nullify labor justice. [...] A regular working schedule... is hard to recover. The company says: 'Come to work, work less today. Come tomorrow.' Imagine when it rains. The worker goes home. And when does the company recover those hours from the worker? On Saturdays. On holidays. On Sundays. (STR 1, Vacaria)

An inspector from the Ministry of Labor, now retired, told me about his ministerial working team.

> Before things were different. It was very different. We were young and well-organized. It wasn't just 'visiting' the fazendas. We investigated. We were organized. We were a team. We planned visits to the companies. While one of us was talking to the owner, a colleague of mine was already entering to check that no employee escaped. Those who were not legally employed ran away. (MPT 3, Porto Alegre)

"Times change rapidly" (STR, Vacaria). The Bolsonaro government has taken a step back, and not all rural unions are particularly active or interested in issues of safety at work. It is, above all, the Fetar-affiliated trade unions that express concerns regarding safety conditions in the workplace. Fetar organizes annual information campaigns about the dangers of work (and about the correct use of tractors, silos and pesticides). It is mostly Fetar-affiliated unions that promote awareness campaigns on workplace safety on local radio stations, in regional meetings with other workers' unions and, when possible, directly with the workers. Interviewees mentioned pesticides: "it is one of the major problems" (STR 1, Vacaria). Fetar has already organized several seminars on the issue of pesticides as well as produced and distributed a booklet on the topic. Also, Fetar leaders are on a state committee organized around this issue.

The president of the Alegrete Union (a municipality in the western region of the state of Rio Grande do Sul) told me the following:

> Last week, we had a very dangerous situation. A farm was burning. There was a product, a pesticide. And the pesticides for growing rice are very strong. All studies are somehow biased. Until we know that product causes cancer [...] who knows how long it will take. Masks are not 100% safe. Overalls for protection [...] workers are not always dressed appropriately [...] Young people are inattentive. Poisons can enter the lungs. Can it cause problems? Yes. But I think there are situations and then there are other situations. We have the CEREST [Reference Center for Occupational Health] here in Alegrete, the regional headquarters, but we don't even have any data. (STR, Alegrete)

Since the workforce is highly informal, controlling the use of pesticides becomes even more difficult. For example, Motta (2019) described the poisoning of 74 rural wage laborers in Vacaria. In this case, the workers didn't even know who their employers were and they didn't have any information about the pesticides being used (which would have prevented a more specific diagnosis). According to a statement taken during this police investigation:

> About 74 people were hospitalized in the last nine days, most of them with pain, probably due to intoxication, without being able to say with certainty either the diagnosis or the cause. There is no way to know where people are working, because patients themselves do not mention this; however, it is known that they come from the orchards. (Health professional testimony, police investigation, mid-2000s, cited in Motta, 2019)

Reducing accidents at work is difficult when the union is not committed, when there is no oversight by the Ministry of Labor, with workers who do not report the incidents and in an overly informal labor market.

Bolsonaro's opinion about pesticides and safety is clear: in 2020, 493 pesticides were approved, a number even higher than in 2019. In two years, President Bolsonaro released almost a thousand pesticides, mostly

Chinese. With regard to safety standards, Bolsonaro is even clearer: standards that protect the health of the worker "make the lives of employers, merchants, entrepreneurs, etc. miserable" (Bolsonaro on Twitter, January 6, 2020). Because of the flexibility of Regulatory Standard number 31 (NR 31), which specifically addresses health and safety in agriculture, livestock, forestry, forestry and fishing, only workplaces with more than ten people are required to meet the minimum conditions of comfort, hygiene, health and safety.

> They want rural workers to go back to pooping in the woods, there is no other way to say it. It is absurd that the right is only valid for workplaces with more than 10 workers. It is denying basic human rights. I want to know what importers of Brazilian agricultural production will think of all this. (Contar, Brasília)

When job security policy worsens, working conditions worsen as well.

Getting a Job

The CAGED database is a record of formal employment. For 2019, it identifies more than 80,000 rural workers in Rio Grande do Sul. There are 17,500 *assalariados* working in the agricultural sector in the northwest (i.e., the Serra regions), which is characterized by smaller farms with a more frequent use of agricultural machinery. In the northeast, in the Planalto regions, there are 14,400 *assalariados*. In the central region, around the city of Santa Maria, there are more than 10,000 *assalariados*. In the municipalities of the metropolitan region of Porto Alegre, there are another 12,000. In the Campanha and in the southern region, a region characterized by large fazendas, CAGED reports approximately 28,000 *assalariados*. In total, there are nearly 83,000 *assalariados*. Most of them are concentrated in the Campanha and the southern region, that is, on large plots of land in the Brazilian Pampa. However, Fetar (2019) estimates that formal and informal labor markets are similar in size in Rio Grande do Sul: there is a total amount of around 160,000 salaried workers, half of whom have been hired with no regular work contract.

Motta (2019) suggests that, in Rio Grande do Sul, the combination of high labor informality with fragmented union representation, low levels of education and unfamiliarity with labor rights could favor social dumping mechanisms and produce slave-like conditions at the workplace. Data from the CAGED system show that of the approximately 80,000 rural workers 1000 *assalariados* are illiterate and 14,000 went through no more than five years of elementary school. Even though 18,000 have completed high school, very few have higher education.

The president of the STR in Mostardas explained to me why this level of informality is so worrisome.

> I visit workers in their communities. The majority of rural workers come from these communities. Workers don't like to expose themselves very much. This is a problem. The *patrão* keeps chasing after them. Workers have a temporary contract for the harvest, which must be renewed each year. This is a problem that we have here. The harvest contract starts in September, with the preparation of the soil, and goes on until the harvest. Six months. There are workers who are old enough to retire, but they worked only during the harvest. They have worked for 20 years but, for social security, it's worth only 10 years. Retiring is a problem. They have never had a formal contract! We started working to urge formal hiring in 1993. Then it got better, but even now we have problems. Bosses don't sign the labor book. [...] The first collective agreement in Mostardas was in 1994. With the *convenção* it got better. At that time, fazendas had machinery, harvesters, hundreds of tractors, but there was not one *assalariado* with a formal contract. There was no record of employees. Very few. [...] The first time that farmers received public financing to invest in silos to store rice... in order to receive funding... they had to demonstrate that they hired regular *assalariados* receiving a salary. What happened? A property with 2500 hectares formally had only two employees with a formal contract! The rest... nothing. Now they are using more pesticides and machinery. There are fewer *assalariados*. But the informality continues. (STR, Mostardas)

In addition to hiring where the labor book (*carteira do trabalho*) is signed in compliance with the law, there are various other forms of contracting workers. For example, the so-called *parcerias frias* (false rural partnership agreements) and the *troca de dias* [exchange days], both illegal.

> I'll give you an example. Let's say I am the owner. I have land lying fallow. I'm not cultivating or using it in any way. You want to work here. I give you 20% of the final production. I give you the possibility of working on my land. You work the fields and pay all the costs. This is a real partnership. A fake partnership is something else. I let you use my land, for the entire harvest, and I pay you a salary. I put food on your table. In those months you

don't work, but I pay you a minimum wage. You stay there with your wife, your children. Like an employee. Eating, sleeping, and working. In this case there is no balance. Half of the year you receive basic foodstuffs, but this is not a partnership. You must pay me my costs back. It could even be called slavery. You get stuck on the farm. With a debt. And you work for me for almost nothing. […] The 'troca de dia' is similar: whoever has a field, even small, and is not producing, helps another. 'I help you today, tomorrow as well'. Is it a symmetrical relationship? It is often asymmetrical, and it could produce extreme exploitation. (MPT 2, Porto Alegre)

On January 28, 2021, the National Day to Combat Slave Labor, an operation was carried out across Brazil. In Rio Grande do Sul, the operation took place in Venâncio Aires and Fontoura Xavier, which led to the rescue of three people: a 30-year-old man, a 52-year-old woman and a 19-year-old young man (the last two, who were mother and child, had signs of clear mental disabilities). They had been in a situation analogous to slavery for three years on a tobacco field. These rescue operations are quite complex. Several institutions took part in the rescue: the Ministério Público do Trabalho [Labor Public Prosecutor] (MPT), the Federal Police (PF), the Subsecretaria de Inspeção do Trabalho [Subsecretariat of Labor Inspection] (SIT), the Federal Public Ministry (MPF) and the Defensoria Pública da União [Federal Public Defender's Office] (DPU). A witness who participated in the rescue in Fontoura Xavier reported the following:

> Nobody was paid, but the owner promised to pay them. The wife and child were fully exploited. There was also a very serious problem due to their mental disabilities. They slept beside a container of pesticides. It was a very precarious situation. It was shocking. (MPT 2, Porto Alegre)

In Venâncio Aires, police found another four workers living on the farm without electricity and running water, while having to use a bucket for physiological needs. Their only water source was a well. The workers did not have a formal contract and did not receive any remuneration. However, a rural worker in Venâncio Aires told me that the facts are perhaps more complex than those reported in the newspapers.

> That worker was also an alcoholic. He was homeless. The *patrão* offered him a house. Did the *patrão* try to help him? I don't know the specifics, but the story is more complex. (Rural worker, Venâncio Aires)

There is another, even more grotesque, aspect of this story: the employer was a member of the same *sindicato* that, in theory, had to represent the enslaved *assalariado*. This is the issue of *dual* representation of rural workers by the same union: that is, the *sindicato eclético* issue, which I will discuss later. Anyway, this raises the question: can a *sindicato* simultaneously represent both an employer sued for slavery and the worker who lives in slave-like conditions?

The MPT data regarding slavery in Rio Grande do Sul for the period 2005–2020 include 345 rescues, plus 16 in January and February of 2021 (Martins, 2021). In addition, 2012 was the year that recorded the highest number of people found working in slave-like conditions within the state: there were 59 cases, 41 of which were in apple orchards. In the entire period analyzed within the state, out of all the economic sectors, agriculture had the most people rescued: a total of 169 cases, representing 48.9% of the total (excluding 67 cases in the logging industry). About 12 workers in the rural sector are rescued from conditions analogous to slavery per year in Rio Grande do Sul.

In cases like these, local *sindicatos* are not mentioned in witness statements or in local newspaper articles. So how are workers' unions dealing with this question? In March 2021, 18 workers were rescued from slave-like conditions on a property in Campestre da Serra and Antônio Prado, in the north of Rio Grande do Sul, on the border with the state of Santa Catarina. In October 2020, a woman and her son who lived in Curitibanos (a town in Santa Catarina) lured residents with the false promise that they would receive a daily wage for their work, along with adequate accommodation and a formal contract. When the rural workers arrived in Campestre da Serra and Antônio Prado, they were placed in unsanitary housing, had their identity documents withheld and were forced to work without receiving a salary. They worked in garlic fields and, eventually, harvested onions, beets, carrots and grapes on rural properties in the Serra region. The exploitation took place for four months, until the Federal Police of Lages investigated the case. After that, the police called for the creation of the Special Group for the Rescue of Workers in Slave-Like Conditions (Antonello, 2021).

> Most employees were men (only two were women), less than 30 years old and with little education (at most fifth grade) attracted by the job offer during the pandemic crisis [...] The auditors found that the recruiters threatened the workers, even with the use of a firearm, so that they would keep up

their activities and not flee the property. In addition to not paying for their work, the recruiters settle up employees with food, beverages and personal hygiene products. The price of these products was higher than the market price, causing workers to incur debts that they could not pay. They were also provided with drugs. Of the 18 employees, only two managed to escape the site—one was rescued by his family, who had to pay the amount charged as his debt [...]. The recruiters acted as intermediaries, known as 'gatos', for a farmer in Flores da Cunha who leased land in Campestre da Serra. This farmer was identified as an employer. He was notified and had to pay, in addition to the unpaid wages, severance pay and all other employment benefits, totaling around BRL 150,000. Employees were released to return to their homes in their hometowns. (Antonello, 2021)

This is an extreme case, but as in other situations, unions seem to be completely absent. In an interview with the newspaper *Zero Hora*, the director of the Legal Department of Farsul, Nestor Hein, who represents the fazendeiros, said that all *ruralista* union members are made aware of the situation:

These are isolated cases, not the norm in state [...] we still must take care of these conceptual reinterpretations because, sometimes, they are gross manipulations used to try to inflate statistics. (Martins, 2021)

On the contrary, the data are worrying and may just be the tip of the iceberg.

There are few formal complaints made. Who is making these claims? How does one make a complaint? Fazendeiros don't even let us enter the farms to inspect. (Contar, Brasília)

In February 2021, the Public Prosecutor for Labor of Rio Grande do Sul (MPT-RS) visited a rural property in the municipality of Bento Gonçalves (also in the Serra region), accompanied by the state police and the superintendent of the Regional Labor and Employment Office in order to investigate a complaint regarding work analogous to slavery on a grape plantation. At the site, the inspection found an accommodation, inside a former aviary that was evidently used as living quarters for the workers, according to their investigation. The accommodation did not meet minimum standards of hygiene and comfort and was unsuitable for a human to live in. At the time of inspection, this space was not being used by workers. The police failed to track down the workers and the investigation is still ongoing. The employer was given an order to regularize the situation and documentation of the workers who worked during the grape harvest and to explain the existence of the living premises on his property. The MPT, through the regional office at Caxias do Sul, which oversees Bento Gonçalves, opened a civil inquiry to investigate the facts. What are the workers' unions of Caxias do Sul and Bento Gonçalves doing? As I already mentioned: "We are no longer interested in the *assalariados*' affairs" (STR, Caxias do Sul).

Slave labor is not "gross manipulation". It takes place in a *milieu* of informality and social dumping, despicable wages, poverty and exhausting work, but it is also a consequence of the lack of interest of workers' and employers' unions in the issue (with differences that must be specified). Without (re)reform in labor relations, extreme cases of slave-like working conditions will never disappear. In theory, Farsul and all the other rural unions in the state of Rio Grande do Sul could work to reduce informality through collective agreements by allowing the union to inspect the estâncias and the fazendas or by overseeing layoff procedures at the workers' union offices in order to reduce informality and illegality together. However, in practice, the situation is different, and labor remains highly risky, precarious and lacking oversight.

It suffices to say that salaried rural workers are uninformed about their rights, and police intervene only in response to a formal complaint. It is also difficult to counteract social dumping. In the state of Santa Catarina, especially on the border with Rio Grande do Sul, *sindicatos* are even more precarious, working conditions are worse and there are no collective agreements: poor workers from Santa Catarina migrate to Rio Grande do Sul for better jobs because "they need to work" (STR, Vacaria). Rio Grande do Sul is not isolated, and working conditions also depend on internal and external migratory flows.

References

Antonello, L. (2021, March 4). Dezoito trabalhadores são resgatados de trabalho escravo e tráfico de pessoas na Serra. *Zero Hora*. https://gauchazh.clicrbs.com.br/pioneiro/geral/noticia/2021/03/dezoito-trabalhadores-sao-resgatados-de-trabalho-escravo-e-trafico-de-pessoas-na-serra-cklvieef6003f016ubc3mrk55.html

Fehlberg, M. F., Santos, I. S., & Tomasi, E. (2001). Acidentes de trabalho na zona rural de Pelotas, Rio Grande do Sul, Brasil: um estudo transversal de base populacional. *Caderno de Saúde Pública, 17*(6), 1375–1381.

Fetar. (2019). Acidentes com Máquinas Agrícolas. Alterações nas Normas Regulamentadoras. In *IV Seminário de segurança e saúde do trabalhador rural*. Fetar.

Frantz, T. R., & Silva Neto, B. (2015). A formação histórica dos sistemas agrários do Rio Grande do Sul. In B. S. Neto & D. Basso (Eds.), *Os sistemas agrários do Rio Grande do Sul: análise e recomendações de políticas* (pp. 33–98). Unijuí.

Hodson, R. (2001). *Dignity at work*. Cambridge University Press.

Leal, O. F. (2021). *Os gaúchos: cultura e identidade masculina no pampa*. Tomo Editorial.

Martins, C. (2021, March 17). RS tem média de 22 resgates de pessoas em situação similar ao trabalho escravo por ano. *Zero Horas*. https://gauchazh.clicrbs.com.br/economia/noticia/2021/03/rs-tem-media-de-22-resgates-de-pessoas-em-situacao-similar-ao-trabalho-escravo-por-ano-ckmcbuilb0051016un60dzmyc.html

Motta, G. (2019). Trabalho Assalariado e Trabalhadores Indígenas nos Pomares de Maçã no Sul do Brasil. *Unpublished doctoral dissertation*. Instituto de Filosofia e Ciências Sociais, Universidade Federal do Rio de Janeiro.

Oliveira, C. V. (2020). Análise de mudanças da cobertura e uso do solo no Bioma Pampa com matrizes de transição. *Unpublished Dissertação de mestrado*. Universidade Federal do Rio Grande do Sul. http://hdl.handle.net/10183/217492

Rodrigues, O. K., Fleischmann, R. U., & Ferreira dos Santos, A. A. (2019). Subnotificação de Acidentes do Trabalho com Morte no Estado do Rio Grande do Sul em 2016: Discrepâncias das Estatísticas Previdenciárias Oficiais. *Revista Escola Judicial do TRT4, 1*(1), 151–180.

Strauss, A., & Corbin, J. (1998). *Basics of qualitative research: Grounded theory procedures and techniques* (2nd ed.). Sage.

CHAPTER 3

Aspects of Rural Unionism

Abstract The legal principles of rural trade unionism are discussed in this chapter. The case of workers' unions, their social function and, above all else, the collective bargaining system are reviewed in detail. Some contradictions that shape the Brazilian labor relations system are also examined in this chapter.

Keywords Rural workers' unions • Service unionism • Collective bargaining

Although Law 13.467/17 altered more than 200 provisions within Brazilian labor law, the Consolidação das Leis Trabalhistas [Consolidation of Labor Law] (CLT) continues to place trade unions under a significant degree of state oversight and intervention (Souto Maior & Severo, 2017; Galvão et al., 2019). Law 13.467/17, for instance, maintains the *unicidade sindical*, a legal principle according to which representation of every category of worker is compulsory and exercised by a single union, which prevents the creation of new *sindicatos*. Also, collective bargaining continues to be limited to the local level (usually by *município* or, at most, extended to one or a few neighboring cities) and by the professional sector. As suggested by Cook (2007), this model of labor relations leads to fragmented representation and the scattered diffusion of *sindicatos*.

Law 13.467/17 removed important pillars of the (already precarious) Brazilian *state corporatism* model of industrial relations. Firstly, the main source of funding for trade unions, the *imposto sindical*—the payment of union dues by the employees, which until 2017 was compulsory and automatically deducted from workers' salaries—henceforth becomes optional (Art. 579). Secondly, the labor reform removed the guarantee that workers were exempt from court fees when filing claims in the labor justice system (Art. 790) and drastically reduced the number of ongoing labor-related hearings. Finally, the labor reform altered the system of collective bargaining and allowed negotiated agreements to override conditions set by labor legislation (Art. 611-A). Thus, the logic of collective negotiation was turned upside down: by reducing labor rights under the law, significant advances in favor of the worker can occur only through negotiating better terms.

The "union tax" is now called "union contribution" (Art. 578) and its deduction is "conditioned to the previous and express authorization of the people who belong to a given professional or economic category or liberal profession" (Art. 579, 582, 583). In Brazil, the end of the *imposto sindical* resulted in a loss of approximately 85% of revenue for the unions: from BRL 3.64 billion in 2017 to BRL 500 million in 2018. Just in relation to Brazilian workers' unions, the amount collected went from BRL 2.24 billion in 2017 to BRL 207.6 million in 2018. The reduction that occurred within employers' unions was lower: from BRL 806 million to BRL 207.6 million. Brazilian unions have been forced to sell off part of their properties, fire their employees, limit their activities and reduce their provision of social services (Freire, 2018; Ribeiro da Costa, 2019). Additionally, when unions began to deliberate in workers' assemblies the maintenance of a minor, alternative trade union contribution via collective agreement, the Bolsonaro administration implemented a decree-law in March 2019 (MP 873), which remained in force until June 28, 2019, to preclude such contributions. However, the MP 873 did not become law due to litigation and political mobilization taken up by the unions, and therefore the decree-law did not permanently take effect.

Before the labor reform, when unions failed to reach a new agreement, the existing agreement would remain valid beyond its contractually stipulated term (i.e., the ultra-activity legal principle). Law 13.467 alters this principle: "Art. 614 - § 3° A collective agreement may not remain in effect for more than two years, with ultra-activity being prohibited". Thus, ultra-activity is no longer permitted by law and the validity of collective agreements are valid only during the period specified within the contract, which can be no greater than two years. However, the legal issue is rather complex, to the point where the Supreme Federal Court (STF) ruled on the constitutionality of article 614 in June 2021. Avoiding this impasse generated by the labor reform is now up to trade unions to improve working conditions via collective bargaining, but "it takes two to tango": workers' and employers' unions must join forces in their negotiations.

Labor reform also created the contractual model of "temporary labor", under which employees must wait to be called up by their employers. If they are called up and accept the job but fail to show up, they must pay a fine to their employers (Art. 452-A). Of course, if they show up, they will only receive payment for the hours they worked. Therefore, there is the possibility that workers may be hired and not work for over a month, during which time they do not receive any wages. Moreover, temporary workers are not entitled to any paid vacation, a clear violation of article 7 of the Constitution.

Labor reform allows for an increase in working hours under individual agreements, leading to 12-hour, or longer, working days without any breaks. Also, Law 13.467 revoked §§ 1 and 3 of article 477 of the CLT, which released companies from the responsibility of having worker layoffs approved at the workers' union offices. The rule, therefore, is that layoffs no longer need to be reviewed by the workers' union. This review can be required only if included in a collective agreement. Obviously, labor reform has had repercussions on collective bargaining practices. When a professional class is not unionized and the unions are divided, there is room for further degradation of workers' rights. In addition to the rules, there are informal relationships, which are difficult to report, in the agricultural sector.

> In our collective agreement, it is clear. There is a clause that requires that the union review layoffs but the *patrão* tells the worker: 'don't go to the union, we can solve it, in our office'. (Contar, Brasília)

Similar to the entire system of Brazilian unionism, the legal system under which the rural unions of Rio Grande do Sul operate has become less stable, which further weakens labor's position. At this point, each rural workers' union decides how to approach labor representation in this new legal scenario, according to their reduced means and moral and political inclinations: unions decide whether to really represent rural workers with fewer resources and more effort required or they choose to take a step back, avoiding many concerns.

The *Sindicatos de Trabalhadores Rurais*

About 400 rural workers' unions are active in Rio Grande do Sul, a state consisting of 497 *municípios*. Rural workers' unions are affiliated to one of three union federations present in Rio Grande do Sul: Fetag, Fetar and Fetraf. It is important to take into consideration that, under the current legislation, unions cannot be members of two federations at the same time. Fetag (Federation of Agricultural Workers in Rio Grande do Sul) has the greatest number of constituent unions at the state level, with 321 *sindicatos* (Picolotto, 2014; Favareto, 2006). However, Fetag is dedicated primarily to family farmers and not to the *assalariados*.

> Fetag no longer represents *assalariados* since 2015. Before, we represented them. Nowadays, Fetar represents the *assalariados* in Rio Grande do Sul. […] Everything relevant to the *assalariados* is with Fetar. […] We work with them. (Fetag, Porto Alegre)

A significant number of Fetag-affiliated *sindicatos* continue to represent *assalariados*, but they are members of a federation that is solely dedicated to family farming. This is a complex topic, which I will explain later in this chapter. The other two federations combined have a lower number of affiliate *sindicatos*. Fetar (the Federation of Rural Salaried Workers in Rio Grande Sul) is solely dedicated to the *assalariados*. Only eight *sindicatos* in Rio Grande do Sul are Fetar-affiliated, but Fetar attends to other local Sindicatos de Trabalhadores Rurais (STRs)—both those affiliated to the Fetag and those affiliated to the Fetar—in collective bargaining practices. Also, Fetraf (the Federation of Workers in Family Farming) is dedicated exclusively to family farmers, like Fetag, and represents about 40 *sindicatos*, the majority of which are dedicated to family farmers.

Fetar was created in 2015, 52 years after the creation of Fetag. Eight unions previously affiliated to Fetag decided to create a federation that deals specifically with *assalariados*: Bagé, Vacaria, São Borja, Arroio Grande, Santa Vitória do Palmar, Itaqui, Santana do Livramento and Uruguaiana. This separation into two federations was not a part of a deliberate plan but came about as a consequence of a ministerial note regarding rural workers' representation. Nelson Wild, who was already Fetag's vice-president, became Fetar's president (and until the end of February 2016 he maintained both titles). In his speech during Fetar's founding congress, Wild reminded those in attendance that it was in Bagé in 1985 that the first collective agreement was signed. Over time, an ever-increasing number of workers were taken out of informality, gaining access to healthcare, security, food and discounted housing, which led to improvements in their quality of life. Wild made assurances that his accumulated experience dealing with this issue in Fetag during the previous 30 years would give him the necessary skills to lead the new rural workers' federation. During the same congress the president of the Fetag, Carlos Joel da Silva, said that the two federations, Fetag and Fetar, "will work together aiming for the well-being of rural workers, whether they are family farmers or rural wage earners" and that "the moment is not time to split but a chance to build" (Rachelle, 2015). After that, however, things turned out a little differently.

While Fetag and Fetar both remain affiliated to the same national trade union federation (the Central dos Trabalhadores e Trabalhadoras do Brasil [CTB]), the third federation operating in Rio Grande do Sul, Fetraf, is affiliated with Central Única dos Trabalhadores (CUT). Fetraf mainly represents family farmers, especially in the Planalto regions.

> We have about 40 *sindicatos*, between workers' unions and associations. We mainly deal with family farming. Family farming is our history. But I must admit that many farmers are hiring *assalariados*. (Fetraf, Aratiba)

> Fetraf only deals with family farming. Especially in the north of the state. We try to organize ourselves in this region. We have few projects in common with the other federations. We share very little with Farsul, almost nothing: we both defend a better retirement pension condition for the farmer. However, we consider the family farmer a worker, not an entrepreneur. It is a very different view from Farsul. Indeed, on all other issues, such as the quality of products, the use of pesticides, government policies, we are totally opposed. Farsul considers family farming on the same level as the landowner. It is not the same. Of course, family farming also hires the *assalariados*. But there aren't many cases because human work tends to be replaced by agricultural machinery. Our history is different. It is also different from the Contag. (Fetraf, Erechin)

The STR in Mostardas, in the southern region, is one of the few Fetraf-affiliated unions engaged with rural salaried workers. As the union's president explained to me, the *sindicato* in Mostardas represents solely those *assalariados* working in Mostardas. In other cases, the union represents workers from several cities.

> In this region we have a *sindicato* in Tavares, and another here in Mostardas. And there are others that are extensions of the *sindicato* in Osório. Major unions in this region are affiliated with Fetag. Maybe Osório will join Fetar, the federation dissident from Fetag […] We have a different way of looking at union issues. The point is that most *sindicatos* are not involved with wage earners. For example, in Tavares there isn't a collective agreement. There, the salary for a rural worker is linked to the minimum salary fixed by the state. Sometimes they use our agreement as a reference. We negotiate every year. We get involved. In Tavares, rural workers have no other labor rights: they don't have a collective agreement and thus no contractual clauses that improve their working conditions. In Palmares, yes, they have a *convenção coletiva* [collective agreement] because the Osório union held a collective agreement and Palmares is included in Osório representation. Palmares is an 'extension' of Osório. […] We are not only concerned with collective bargaining but also with the health of the worker. For example, the issue of pesticides. (STR, Mostardas)

In order to reach a collective agreement, each STR must be authorized by a *carta sindical* [union charter] issued by the Minister of Labor. At the moment, most of these *sindicatos* are *sindicatos ecléticos*, which are workers' unions, and *carta sindical*, which represent two distinct professional categories: family famers and salaried rural workers. Both were included, until 2014, within a single rural workers' union. The *carta sindical* details the two categories that the STR can represent. This "double" representation has created debates and controversies over time that are destined to grow: which group is being represented by a STR? Is it the *assalariados*, the family farmers, or both, as has been the case in the past?

The issue was unsettled until the Ministry of Labor issued a clarification through *nota técnica* [technical note] n. 88 of 2014. The consensus toward a new normative framework for rural salaried workers was consolidated based on Decree-Law no. 1166, of April 15, 1971 (where the differences between rural salaried and family farmers was originally defined). Subsequently, *nota técnica* n. 88 allowed the dissolution of the so-called "eclectic category of rural worker" into the separate categories of "rural salaried workers" (i.e., the *assalariados*) and "family farmers" (Picolotto, 2014, 2018; Brazil, 2014). However, until a few years ago, the separation of rural salaried workers and family farmers through the formation of another specific trade union system mainly took place at the confederation (Contag and Contar) or federation (Fetag and Fetar) level. On the other hand, about 130 rural *sindicatos* representing local employers—fazendeiros, large landowners and farmers—are affiliated only with Farsul (Federação da Agricultura do Estado do Rio Grande do Su): capital is clearly united while labor is divided.

The issue is certainly controversial. While *sindicatos* have tended to remain eclectic until recently, a growing group of Fetag-affiliated unions in the last few years have been attempting to change their statutes so that they represent only family farmers: these rural unions are no longer STR; they become STAFs (Sindicatos dos Trabalhadores da Agricoltura Familiar) [Family Farming Workers' Unions]. The 400 workers' unions present in Rio Grande do Sul are now divided between STRs and STAFs: while most of the unions in Rio Grande do Sul remain STRs, a growing number, especially in the Serra and central regions, have decided to no longer represent *assalariados* and therefore become STAF. At the moment, there are 37 STAF in Rio Grande do Sul. Union sources and interviews indicate a recent turning point: many Fetag-affiliated unions no longer want to represent *assalariados*.

Some questions come to mind: who is representing the *assalariados* in those municipalities where there is no longer an STR? Considering these recent trends, do all STRs sign collective agreements? Is the *sindicato eclético*—representing both salaried workers and family farmers (i.e., employees and employers)—a contradiction? Do unions that remain STRs and are affiliated with either Fetag or Fetraf truly represent *assalariados*?

It is also evident that there are different and divergent positions on this point, even between unions belonging to the same federation. Fetag and Fetag-affiliated unions report the following:

> All the unions in the region are trying to become STAFs. This is the trend. (STR, Antônio Prado)

> This eclectic union system is not working at all. (STR, Venâncio Aires)

> In December 2020, we successfully modified our union charter (*carta sindical*). Now we only represent family farmers. Unions in the region no longer want to represent wage earners. [...] We had a union charter that allowed us to sign *convenções coletivas* but we never signed a specific collective agree-

ment for the *assalariados*. We provide counseling in the case of dismissal, but in just a few cases. (STR, Caxias do Sul)

Since 2015, we don't represent the *assalariados* anymore. The trend is to become STAF. I don't know exactly how many STRs are changing their charters. (Fetag, Porto Alegre)

In meetings with other workers' unions in the region, there is a lot of discussion about becoming a STAF. 'Why?' I ask. We have rural salaried workers here. Why don't we represent *assalariados* anymore? If we (a Fetag-affiliated union) don't represent the *assalariados*, who will represent them? If we decide to end double representation ... who represents the *assalariados*? [...] And we also provide them with medical assistance. (STR, Flores da Cunha)

Since 2015, we decided to no longer represent the *assalariados*. This was decided by the union before I began working here. At the moment, we are changing our charter. Now, the Ministry of Labor should approve our new status and change the union's charter. (STR, Santa Cruz do Sul)

We have never signed a collective agreement. Also, we recently changed the statute: now we only represent family farming. (STAF, Canguçu)

Fetar and Fetar-affiliated unions report the following:

There is this question of the eclectic union. It makes the entire system [of labor relations] difficult. (Fetar 1, Porto Alegre)

In other Brazilian states, unions clearly are heading towards dissociation. In Rio Grande do Sul, it is a little different. Also, the jurisprudence and the judiciary are not clear at all. They have changed their interpretation over time. You can now even join more than one federation, according to some legal interpretations [...] in any case, I think we took a step forward. Before, the *assalariados* were within the Fetag. Now, after the separation, we have more space. Within the structure of family farming [the Fetag], we did not have enough space. There was just a department dedicated to the *assalariados*. Now we have a federation. Do we need to move forward in Rio Grande do Sul? Advance more decisively? Yes, we definitely do, we need to move forward toward creating regional unions to represent *assalariados*. (STR, Arroio Grande)

We are an STR, and we must reduce conflicts between the two groups. Saturday, I was in Bagé. I was attending an assembly of employers who build fencing. There was an associate of ours who had hired three employees without signing their *carteiras de trabalho* [work book]. One of them gets injured. A pretty deep cut. What do I tell his employer? The employee needs a formal contract, and his employer has to sign his *carteira de trabalho*. Nothing happened. [...] Both the employer and the employee are members of our union. So, we sought to reach an agreement between the two and get the employee's *carteira de trabalho* signed. They reached an agreement without signing his *carteira*. It was very expensive for the employer to resolve. The two are members of the same union. We must manage conflicts, but we don't always succeed. (STR, Bagé)

The situation is troubling throughout the state. There are municipalities where there are many *assalariados* without a collective agreement. (STR, Vacaria)

It is therefore a real and complex scenario with different logics of mobilization, political values and union histories. "There are too many differences [...] it's too complicated to continue like this" (STR, Santa Vitória do Palmar). These differences, however, combine with the contradictions of the Brazilian system of labor regulation and these institutional pressures are internalized at the level of individual unions. Now, it is the union itself, every single union, that decides how to deal with these different dilemmas.

Collective Bargaining

Collective bargaining takes place between two unions at the local level: an STR (workers' union) bargains to reach a collective agreement with the local employers' union (the *sindicato ruralista*). Farsul supports its affiliated *sindicatos ruralistas* while Fetar backs every single STR that actually makes an effort to sign a collective agreement, regardless of whether they are affiliated with Fetar. If an agreement between the two *sindicatos* is not reached, a labor judge resolves the dispute and determines the contents of the collective agreement. The latter takes place only if the workers' union takes the employers' union to court.

There are 120 active collective agreements in Rio Grande do Sul, but this leaves a large part of the state's territory uncovered. This means that not all STRs reach collective agreements. Out of the 497 municipalities in Rio Grande do Sul, 34.6% are covered by a collective agreement while

65.4% are not. It is important to analyze these data, considering the number of rural workers within the municipalities of the region. In the southern regions (the South and the Campanha), which are composed of municipalities that are characterized by large land holdings and a significant presence of *assalariados*, the percentage of cities that are covered by collective bargaining agreements is significantly higher. On the other hand, in the northern, central and eastern regions, this percentage is drastically lower. These municipalities are characterized by small land ownership and a lower number of rural workers when compared with the *latifundios* of the southern regions. In total, about 60,000 workers are covered by a collective agreement (72.7%) while 22,500 are not (27.3%).

> There are about 120 conventions in force in Rio Grande do Sul. We have the southern region, the border region and the central one, where a majority of salaried workers are concentrated. We started to sign conventions in the border region, then we began covering more regions but there are still regions that do not have coverage, such as the Serra. In Rio Grande do Sul, we have around 200,000 rural employees, and we represent maybe 75% of those workers, not even 80% of rural employees. […] We even have some situations… where there is no employers' union and we negotiate directly with Farsul, the employers' federation. Where there is no negotiation and no agreement, the state legal minimum wage, fixed by the law, is in force. Until 2001, the minimum wage did not exist. Since then, those who don't have a current collective agreement receive only the minimum wage. But the big problem in our state is still informality in the labor market, which is huge, and after the labor reform and the dismantling of the Ministry of Labor informality has increased a lot. (Fetar 1, Porto Alegre)

It is also true that the smaller presence of *assalariados* in a *município* would reduce the concern of the local union in reaching a collective bargaining agreement. The CAGED system registers that in 341 municipalities (68.6% out of the total) there are less than 100 regular rural workers. However, in Rio Grande do Sul, 62 *municípios* are not covered by a collective agreement despite there being more than 100 active rural workers registered in the *município*. More than half of these cases are in the Serra and the Planalto (see Table 3.1).

> There are cases like Caxias do Sul, which has over a thousand *assalariados* that are regularly hired, but who knows how many informal ones […] for whom there is no collective agreement. (STR, XX)

I would like to know why, in Canguçu, which has more than a thousand *assalariados*, they do not reach a collective agreement. What prevents them from making a collective agreement? (STR, X)

A descriptive analysis and a multiple correspondence analysis suggest some answers to the previous questions (Di Franco, 2006). As explained in the methodological notes in this text's introduction, I collected data directly from *sindicatos* and complemented these data with ministerial sources. The percentage of agreements present in the municipalities of Rio Grande do Sul is distributed by region (the p value for the chi-square test is significant). Table 3.1 explains in detail this non-homogeneous distribution of collective agreements among the regions of Rio Grande do Sul.

I also performed a multiple correspondence analysis in order to confirm my qualitative findings and to obtain a more detailed overview among four nominal variables: (1) federation (three categories: Fetag; Fetar; Fetraf); (2) regions (five categories: Planalto; Serra; central region; metropolitan region of Porto Alegre; Pampa); (3) rural workers (the number of

Table 3.1 Presence of a *convenção coletiva* [collective agreement] in the municipalities of Rio Grande do Sul (cross-tabulation)

	Collective agreement		Total
	Yes	No	
Northwest (Planalto)	60	156	216
	27.80%	72.20%	100%
Northeast (Serra)	13	41	54
	24.10%	75.90%	100%
Western Central region (Central region)	22	9	31
	71.00%	29.00%	100%
Eastern Central region (Central region)	10	44	54
	18.50%	81.50%	100%
Metropolitan region of Porto Alegre	27	71	98
	27.60%	72.40%	100%
Southwest (Pampa/Campanha)	18	1	19
	94.70%	5.30%	100%
Southeast (Pampa/South region)	22	3	25
	88%	12%	100%
	172	325	497
	34.60%	65.40%	100%

$p < 0.000$

rural salaried workers in each municipality; four categories: 0–50 rural salaried workers; 51–100; 101–300; above 301); (4) collective agreement (presence of a legal *convenção coletiva*; two categories: yes; no). Only the first two factors of the multiple correspondence analysis have been considered (84.7% of the total variance is explained by the model): the first dimension explains 54.4% while the second one explains 30.4%. The first dimension discriminates above all the *number of assalariados*, the *presence of a collective agreement* and the regions.

Figure 3.1 corresponds closely to what I observed in my interviews. The proximity of two categories, in Fig. 3.1, observed in relation to the two dimensions indicates a large, positive correlation between categories as measured by the chi-square test. The category *Fetar* is correlated with *the Pampa* and *>301*, both on dimensions 1 and 2. Fetar-affiliated unions sign collective agreements, and they are most present where there is a greater number of *assalariados*, particularly in the southern region (the Pampa and the Campanha). The category *Fetar* (on the top right) is significantly different from the category *No: Fetar* (on the left). The three federations are positioned in three different quadrants: this indicates different patterns of association between Fetar, Fetag, and Fetraf. The *Fetag* category is close to the categories *No* and *101–300* on both dimensions and is also significantly different from the category *>301*. The *Fetraf* category is close to the categories *No*, *Planalto* and *51–100*, especially in the first dimension. The proximity of the categories *No*, *51–100* and *101–300* on the first dimension, the one which explains the greatest variance, suggests that a significant part of Fetag-affiliated and Fetraf-affiliated unions do not sign collective agreements, a concerning trend for rural unionism.

Negotiating Clauses

The presidents of Fetar-affiliated unions mention a set of limitations that affect collective bargaining. They recall the mechanisms included in Law 13.467 (among all, the prevalence of negotiated terms over legislation) but also specific elements of rural culture (Colvero et al., 2014). Protests are very rare, and it is difficult to visit the fazendas to talk with workers. As many union leaders say: "because of distances in rural areas we can't visit the farms" (STR, Uruguaiana). The presidents of STRs also mention resistance from *sindicatos ruralistas* and Farsul.

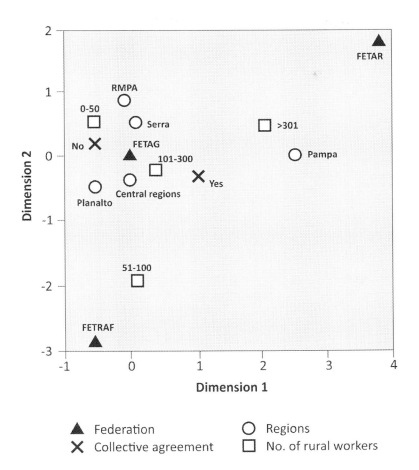

Fig. 3.1 Multiple correspondence analysis plot for dimensions 1 and 2 (categories)

> Nowadays, when you try to include one more clause, the *sindicato ruralista* demands you remove another. And if the *sindicato ruralista* doesn't sign [the *convenção*], it's a problem. (STR, Vacaria)

The current scenario is described below:

> When you enter into a collective agreement, you move towards regular and better work. A series of mechanisms is created which goes beyond the con-

> tract itself: here we are! Workers can also recognize your work, which improves the quality of rural labor. (Fetar 1, Porto Alegre)

> In the event of employee dismissal, the worker can come here to the union to check that everything is in order. This is no longer required by law, but the collective agreement makes it possible and the process remains valid. The STR can check the employee's entire work history to ensure that all labor rights have been respected and that everything is in order. (STR, Quaraí)

> It has become more difficult to negotiate because of labor reform. We have to fight today to recover many clauses that were previously included in the collective agreement. (STR, Alegrete)

After negotiations, the *convenção* has to be approved by the assembly. In most *sindicatos* it is difficult to bring workers together in assemblies to approve the agreement.

> Union assemblies take place with 200/300 workers, but we have 3,000 members. Employers do not give time off for the workers to go out and attend the assembly. We once had 700 workers present in the assemblies, but now there are not even 300. [...] The *latifundios* are very strong here. [The salary] is around BRL 1,200 [in 2019]. With 'hazard pay', it goes up to 1,400 BRL. They have overtime, which the worker confuses with their salary, and then it sometimes goes up to 2,000 or more. But the worker is on the job at least 12 hours during the harvest, working day and night. (STR, Uruguaiana)

> Workers do not show up to the assembly. What can we do? (STR, Venâncio Aires)

As reported in the interviews, when there are no other alternatives, the *sindicato* is indeed "seen by the workers as a last resort" (STR, Uruguaiana). In other words, even when a union is frequently active, the political culture of the countryside does not favor unionism or collective mobilization. Rural labor relations occur within this *social milieu*. The absence of strikes and protests also negatively impacts collective bargaining: without worker engagement or strikes, the *convenção* process is limited to a set of formal meetings that take place between workers' and employers' representatives.

Throughout Uruguaiana's history, we had only one work stoppage, with 17 workers on a farm, [...] The quarrel with the *fazendeiro* was all about wages and productivity. (STR, Uruguaiana)

No, in our rural areas there has never been a strike; the settlers are the ones who strike. Sometimes we join them. The employee comes here and complains to the *sindicato* and we listen and seek to negotiate on their behalf. (STR 2, Santana do Livramento)

In the countryside it is difficult to have one [a strike]. [It is difficult] to gather a large group of workers. This is because of the distance between the *fazenda* and town. Something changed a few years ago. Now, because of collective agreements, there are not as many complaints [...] if you respect the agreement, you avoid complaints [...] then, it calmed down a little, and when *sindicatos* are more active there is less informality. (Fetar 1, Porto Alegre)

Strike? I have never participated in one. (Rural worker 3, Vacaria)

As far as I can remember, I have never gone on strike. We *assalariados* are a bit timid. (Rural worker, Mostardas)

Unfortunately, *Sistema Mediador* (http://www3.mte.gov.br/sistemas/mediador/ConsultarInstColetivo) does not provide access to all of the *conveções* signed in Rio Grande do Sul. However, out of a sample of 40 it was possible to observe the most important clauses included in *convenções coletivas*. Collective agreements are typically similar with no significant differences either between regions or over time. Company-wide agreements are also very rare.

The most pronounced regional difference involves the collective agreements of *assalariados* who work in the soy fields of the southern region, which tend to be more generous. Even so, wages remain extremely low. Collective bargaining leads to a wage higher than the state minimum and generally adjusts for inflation. Most collective agreements involve significant wage readjustments, approximately 4% of the base salary. At the end of the first half of 2021, Fetar had reached a 90% renewal of collective labor agreements (the remaining conventions have their renewal in July and August of 2021). The 2021 negotiations have shown increases in real wages above 0.5%, adjusting for inflation with the INPC (National Consumer Price Index) as a reference (Fetar 2, Porto Alegre).

The 2020 collective agreements are very similar to those from 2019, which in turn are similar to those signed in 2018: after the 2017 labor reform, workers' unions have tried to preserve achievements reached prior to the reform.

Collective agreements are extremely important for rural unions. The *convenção coletiva* makes union financing possible because of "union confederative contribution"; it allows unions to conduct spot inspections at fazendas and give workers time off when there is a trade union meeting or assembly. Also, clauses included in the *convenção coletiva* make it possible for layoffs to continue being reviewed by the union.

Analyzing the collective agreements, I routinely found clauses about participation in the assembly, even if such participation is not respected. In almost all the *convenções* there is a clause regarding union dues. However, the so-called "confederative contribution" is less than previously obligatory union dues, and, in any case, it is always voluntary. The worker can also recover the amount after a formal request sent to the union. In most collective agreements, the amount paid for food and accommodation is established: it is important to fix costs, which cannot be excessive, to avoid a real dependence of the eventually indebted worker on the employer.

In addition to the clauses just mentioned, collective agreements always contain other significant clauses; for example, the addition of hazard pay (which increases the salary by about 10%) and funeral benefits (in the event of an employee's death, his family receives an amount equivalent to a month's minimum wage).

Other clauses are present in half of the collective agreements I analyzed. The so-called *quadriênio* is important to raise the salary: when an *assalariado* completes four years of work with the same company or fazenda, he is entitled to a 5% increase in his salary. While not always respected, such a fundamental clause (which may or may not be present) allows the worker to review the terms of his dismissal with the union, where the *sindicato* checks the worker's entire history on that job, including his paychecks, and eventually requests severance pay from the employer. In half of the contracts I reviewed, the job titles and corresponding salaries were diversified. For example, the foreman (*capataz*) has a higher base salary.

In one out of every five contracts, there is a clause about the union's ability to conduct site inspections at farms, something that is rarely honored by the fazendeiros. Less frequent is a bonus for working nights (present in one of every three agreements). In one out of ten *convenções*, there is a transport assistance clause for the rural worker as well as support to pay for their children's day care.

Clauses such as the *bank of hours* or the *doma* (taming of horses) are important but much less common. In the case of the *doma*, when a rural worker tames a horse, he earns the equivalent of a month's minimum wage. Without a clause like this, horse training would be required by the fazendeiro without the worker receiving additional compensation. However, the price for taming a horse by hiring a professional on the market is two to three times higher than the minimum wage.

In few contracts there are also clauses about extra food given for productivity, usually rice or meat. Employee participation in company profits is rare.

There are a few clauses in the *convenções* that involve social benefits. For example, the 25th clause of the convention in force in Santa Vitória do Palmar on the recognition of medical certificates to justify the worker's absence says that "employers will recognize as valid medical and dental certificates given by professionals who provide services to the STR of Santa Vitória do Palmar"; these clauses, specific but limited to medical certification, are found in very few *convenções*. In terms of safety in the workplace, collective agreements contain few clauses. These clauses are difficult to negotiate and it is almost impossible to control how they are implemented. Additionally, the *convenção* rarely discusses workplace safety issues, which are mostly limited to the employer's obligations to providing a medical kit containing first aid for injured employees: "we try to put these clauses inside the agreement but there is resistance […] also, do they really apply them?" (STR, Uruguaiana).

As mentioned previously, work in rural areas is not safe. With the reduction of public resources available for the SUS [Unified Health System] (Brazil's public healthcare system) together with increased demand for medical care, attempts to include clauses on safety in the collective agreement are natural. For example, in Uruguaiana:

> Employers almost always want to include only economic clauses, and even these only with great difficulty. They just want to ignore inflation. They mainly refuse to put in clauses that include penalties: we can never put something like 'if this happens, then that will happen'; it is only left up to what is in the existing legislation. The same thing happens with workplace safety conditions. Another example is that the law obliges the boss to provide harnesses, which is the equipment for riding horses, but there is no clause that

says what will happen if they are not provided; then if it goes to the courts and nothing is solved, it ends up as a dead clause. (STR, Uruguaiana)

Collective bargaining does not allow significant alternatives other than those established under the current legislation. Bargaining at the regional level, rather than at the municipal level, could change the logic of collective bargaining and therefore the contents of collective agreements, but:

> I've said it a thousand times: negotiation at the regional level. Perhaps it would improve the content of collective agreements [...] Nowadays, bargaining is increasingly difficult [...] We hold the assemblies and start trying to reserve meetings with employers and sometimes they don't answer for a month. We always meet them there, and there is a lot of resistance. (STR, 2, Santana do Livramento)

> We are looking for a new collective agreement model. We are thinking about reaching regional collective agreements or even a single collective agreement for the state of Rio Grande do Sul. (Fetar 2, Porto Alegre)

Generally, the relations between the workers' union and the employers' union are not conflictual, but neither are they collaborative. Often these relationships begin and end during the collective agreement renewal process. In rarer cases, the two unions meet regularly.

> I regularly meet the President of the *sindicato ruralista*. When there is a problem, we discuss it. So, I also discuss with employers. I'll give you an example. At a recent event, a worker contacts us: the accommodation where he was living, on the *fazenda*, was in poor condition. We talked with the fazendeiro. 'Let's discuss the matter!' And the fazendeiro fixes his housing without hesitation and without argument. The relationship can also be peaceful. [...] What is found in the *convenção* is only part of the relations between unions. (STR, Arroio Grande)

It is also possible that workers' unions have jurisdiction over different territory than the rural workers' unions: that is, the two union charters (*carta sindical*) are different in terms of what municipalities they cover. These asymmetries make collective bargaining difficult.

> The *carta sindical* of the local *sindicato ruralista* is different from ours and covers different municipalities. So, it's a problem. These days a case hap-

pened to me. I almost reported it to the public Ministry of Labor. We have a *convenção* here in the city of XXX. Our base is in XXX but we have a branch in a neighboring city. But the *ruralista* union don't. With whom do we sign the agreement? Do we have to sign it with another rural union that has responsibility over that municipality? (STR, XXX)

We have a union charter. We can sign a collective agreement. But there is no rural union here in Flores da Cunha. So, we must ask the *ruralista* union in Caxias do Sul to sign a *convenção* with us. But they aren't interested in signing a collective agreement with us. (STR, Flores da Cunha)

In summary, in Flores da Cunha there is a workers' union (Fetag-affiliated) with a union charter but there is no corresponding employers' union (*sindicato ruralista*). The *ruralista* union with jurisdiction over the municipality is based in neighboring Caxias do Sul. There is no active collective agreement in Flores da Cunha or even in Caxias do Sul, where the president of the local STR (Fetag-affiliated) is not at all interested in representing the *assalariados*, just family farmers. What catches my attention is that Valmir Susin, president of the employers' union of Caxias do Sul (which is affiliated with Farsul), was already president of the STR of Caxias do Sul. He moved from the union of rural workers to chair the union representing the employer.

Respondents also cite cases in which unions that represent a different category of employees negotiate with the *sindicato ruralista*.

In this region, the food workers' union deals with collective agreements. We don't sign collective agreements. They negotiate directly with the *ruralista* employers' union. (Fetraf, Aratiba)

In some municipalities in the region, it is the food trade workers' union that signs the collective agreement for rural workers. What a mess! (STR, Venâncio Aires)

Providing Services

When I enter the premises of a *sindicato*, one striking aspect is the presence of medical clinics there. Behind the reception door, in addition to the offices of the union leaders, where compliance with the collective agreement is discussed, I generally observe a waiting room and a dentist's office, a general practitioner, a gynecologist and sometimes even a psychologist.

Medical assistance is present in all Fetar-affiliated and most Fetag-affiliated unions. Especially in the most isolated towns where public health services are even more precarious, the medical assistance service offered by the union to rural workers and their relatives is indispensable. Therefore, much of the physical space of the unions is occupied by rooms reserved for medical care.

> We have a doctor here, for us, on Wednesdays and Thursdays; we also have an agreement with doctors here in the town center. A general practitioner comes here. Workers don't pay, and the doctor brings some medicine for free. Also, depending on the medicine, we have an agreement at a pharmacy. And in case the doctor cannot resolve the issue, she refers us to a specialist. We had an agreement for surgeries where the workers paid the amount in three installments, and hospitalization, if necessary, is free. [...] A week ago, an injured worker arrived here at the *sindicato*. He had injured his leg, and he asks me: 'what do I do?' We told him to go to the hospital. We provide services but the *sindicato* is not a hospital. In these cases, we provided all the documentation necessary for the diagnosis. (STR 1, Santana do Livramento)

> Here at the *sindicato* we offer medical assistance for the employee and his or her family. We cover the whole family, regardless of how many children. We offer routine medical care. We provide dental that covers 50% of the treatment. We also provide good discounts in clinical laboratories [...] We have many agreements with clinics. Our health system here in town is excellent, but there are tests that cannot be conducted here: for example, an ultrasound is very expensive. There's only one doctor. Often, the discount that we get in Uruguaiana or Livramento is already significant. We have agreements with all rural unions. If a worker lives here and needs help in Alegrete, we invite him to contact the rural union in Alegrete. (STR, 1, Quaraí)

> We use the services, here at the union. Dentist, doctor. When we need to... we go to the *sindicato*. We wait for our turn and the doctor meets with us. My husband is also allowed to use these services, and my son too. (Rural worker 4, Vacaria)

> I am here with my son. I'm taking him to the dentist. [...] I'm a union member. The dentist is quite cheap. (Rural worker 2, Vacaria)

Rural unions perform social services that go beyond mere wage negotiation. The STR in Santo Antônio da Patrulha provides counseling for family farmers, even though it doesn't represent rural workers in collective bargaining. In Santo Antônio, there is no active collective agreement; however, some rural salaried workers are union members, and they receive medical assistance.

> Today we have 70 rural salaried workers. We have a doctor and healthcare for them, [but] there is no collective bargaining. I say that with a sense of self-criticism. (STR, Santo Antônio da Patrulha)

The tension between class and service unionism is evident. However, when locally available medical care is precarious—or even non-existent—rural unions tend to provide basic medical care services. It has therefore not been possible to close the local *sindicato* to the public during the COVID-19 pandemic: "it would represent a retaliation against rural workers" (rural worker, Santana do Livramento).

Because of the labor reform that ended mandatory union contributions and other provisional measures adopted by Bolsonaro's administration—which made it even more difficult to collect union contributions—workers' loyalty is fundamental. A larger number of members ensure that there is adequate funding, which also guarantees the continuity of social assistance provided by the rural unions. The relationship of trust between trade union contribution and social protection is now indissociable:

> From the signing of the collective agreement, the worker has up to 90 days to request back his union dues, but usually no one comes here to request it back. Sometimes it's the employer's office who comes, not the worker. Some bosses come here and say they didn't collect the worker's dues. Our union employees can even check whether the company has paid or not. Then the worker takes up this issue and the company starts to collect. So, we can provide medical assistance. [...] We have two doctors: BRL 40 for each medical appointment. A doctor who treats patients here in town usually charges BRL 300 [...] We have free medication. Free dental care, and BRL 20 for dependents. [...] Medical care should not be the responsibility of the union. The role of the union should be different. But we're in a country where we have nothing. The cost of doctors and dentists that treat patients here in the union is half of our total costs [of the union structure]. We spend BRL 100,000 a month. That's a lot. (STR 1, Vacaria)

Even though I was unable to obtain statewide data on the union system in Rio Grande do Sul, my research shows that in the Fetar-affiliated unions where a collective agreement is in force, which is particularly the case in the southern region and the Campanha, the union also typically provides medical care. In regions where there is no collective agreement, the union usually does not provide these services. In other cases, the STR acts a welfare provider. This begs an important question: what will happen when the STR no longer represents *assalariados*?

> We are ending our representation of the *assalariados* [...] I'm not sure what's going on. We will probably no longer offer medical services to the *assalariados*. Perhaps by paying a fee... (STR, Santa Cruz do Sul)

> We offer services only to our family farming members since we became STAF. A rural *assalariado* no longer receives our services: he should already be or become a family farmer. (STAF, Canguçu)

All the current STAFs were born as STRs and therefore have offered services to both family farmers and *assalariados*. By changing the statute and opting for the representation of just one of these categories, the STAFs effectively exclude *assalariados* from the services provided by the union. It is worth mentioning, however, that there are also unions associated with Fetag that continue to provide medical assistance to the *assalariados*, but those that ended double representation by becoming STAFs no longer provide these services to salaried workers.

A Fetraf-affiliated trade unionist (who in turn is affiliated with CUT, and not CTB, as in the case of Fetag and Fetar) commented that providing health services to workers is outside the realm of union responsibility:

> We do not offer services to our associates. We think it's wrong. The public healthcare system must provide treatment, not the union. We therefore have no agreements with private hospitals, clinics, etc. The state has to take care of it, not the union. (STR, Mostardas)

With regard to the provision of services, there is a relevant difference between unions: on the one hand, workers' unions affiliated with Fetar are more engaged in providing health care services to *assalariados*. On the other hand, the issue of service provision is not considered when an STR becomes an STAF and the *assalariados* lose both union representation and the material provision of vital services.

STAFs and many STRs—especially those affiliated with Fetag—offer targeted services to the small agricultural producer. Family farmers require different services than *assalariados*. While the *assalariado* mainly requires medical services, family farmers also need professional advice:

> We have agronomists who advise [family farmers] on how to invest. We do cost analyses. Our members pay half price. We help with Incra [National Institute of Colonization and Agrarian Reform] registration for the wine companies. We registered 3,000 viticulture sites this year! We take care of social security benefits, sick pay, maternity pay, workman's compensation and retirement. We have a lawyer who helps with contracts, files taxes, and conducts inventory. (STR, Flores da Cunha)

For interviewees, questions about their unions can be rather embarrassing. Only in rare cases did my interviewees reflect on their own union and very few times did they dare to evaluate or express opinions about other unions in Rio Grande do Sul. When other unions come up in conversation, the answers I received often became more nuanced or ambiguous: "that's it", "what to do?", "I don't know what other unions are doing". A question posed by a union leader, reflecting on the changes in Fetag-affiliated unions, raises an important point: "Is this a union or a service company?" (STR, XX).

References

Brazil. (2014). Nota Técnica n. 88. In *Ministério do Trabalho e Emprego. Manual de Procedimentos de Registro Sindical*. MTE.

Colvero, R. B., Paniagua, E. R., & Carbonai, D. (2014). Uruguaina: suas Fronteiras e sua Identidade. *Estudios históricos, 12*, 1–16. http://www.estudioshistoricos.org/12/artigo%20uruguaiana.pdf

Cook, M. L. (2007). *The politics of labour reform in Latin America: between flexibility and rights*. The Pennsylvania State University.

Di Franco, G. (2006). *Corrispondenze multiple e altre tecniche multivariate per variabili categoriali*. Milan, FrancoAngeli.

Favareto, A. (2006). Agricultores, Trabalhadores: os Trinta Anos do Novo Sindicalismo Rural no Brasil. *Revista Brasileira de Ciências Sociais, 21*(62), 27–44. https://doi.org/10.1590/S0102-69092006000300002

Freire, D. (2018, November 23). Em 'agonia', sindicatos demitem e vendem imóveis para sobrevive. *Veja*. https://veja.abril.com.br/economia/em-agonia-sindicatos-demitem-e-vendem-imoveis-para-sobreviver/

Galvão, A., Castro, B., Krein, J. D., & Teixeira, M. O. (2019). Reforma Trabalhista: Precarização do Trabalho e os Desafios para o Sindicalismo. *Caderno CRH, 32*(86), 253–270. https://doi.org/10.9771/ccrh.v32i86.30691

Picolotto, E. L. (2014). A formação de um sindicalismo de agricultores familiares no Sul do Brasil. *Sociologias*, *16*(35), 204–236. https://doi.org/10.1590/S1517452220140 00100008

Picolotto, E. L. (2018). Pluralidade Sindical no Campo? Agricultores Familiares e Assalariados Rurais em um Cenário de Disputas. *Lua Nova: Revista de Cultura e Política*, *104*, 201–238. https://doi.org/10.1590/0102-201238/104

Rachelle, I. (2015). Assalariados rurais têm federação própria. Informativo de Imprensa Fetag n. 1089. http://fetagrs.org.br/assalariados-rurais-tm-federao-prpria/

Ribeiro da Costa, L. A. (2019). A estrutura sindical e a negociação coletiva brasileira nos anos 2000 e os primeiros impactos da Reforma Trabalhista (Lei 13.467/17). *XVI Encontro nacional ABET*. Salvador (BA).

Souto Maior, J. L., & Severo, V. (2017). *Manual da Reforma Trabalhista: Pontos e Contrapontos*. Editora Sensus.

CHAPTER 4

What Is a Rural Union for?

Abstract This chapter explores the contradictions that take place during collective negotiations in the agricultural sector of Rio Grande do Sul. A comparison with the Argentine model is also provided.

Keywords Union representation • COVID-19 pandemic • Comparative analysis

The relationship between rural workers and *sindicatos* is certainly complex: the institutional design of Brazilian trade unionism is local and fragmentary, and rural workers' *sindicatos* are affiliated with three different federations, two different confederations and two central unions. A significant part of workers' unions doesn't sign collective agreements, while another part does not even show interest in collective bargaining or rural workers' representation. Rural unionism is also divided between family farming and wage labor, Sindicato de Trabalhadores Rurais (STR) and Sindicato de Trabalhadores da Agricultura Familiar (STAF), typical class unionism and service unionism, a passionate and exclusive dedication toward the *assalariados* and a more flexible one, which is in some cases hostile to rural workers. Not all rural workers' unions in Rio Grande do Sul are truly committed, and not even their presence guarantees workers'

© The Author(s), under exclusive license to Springer Nature Switzerland AG 2022
D. Carbonai, *Rural Workers, Sindicatos and Collective Bargaining in Rio Grande do Sul*, https://doi.org/10.1007/978-3-030-94808-5_4

representation. Of course, representation occurs with significant differences: namely, Fetar-affiliated unions are more committed.

How can worker representation be improved? Interviewees suggest that organizing a different type of negotiation and collective bargaining (centralized at the regional or state level) and setting up new regional *sindicatos* specifically dedicated to rural salaried workers, among others, would improve labor representation.

In any case, the work in the fields doesn't stop—even during a global pandemic: the *patrão* decides when work can stop and workers' tasks are not dependent on epidemiological contingencies.

The COVID-19 Pandemic

With the advancement of COVID-19, rural workers' union headquarters initially closed for a brief period in Rio Grande do Sul. However, without a state or federal stay-at-home policy, work in the fields continued—and still continues—especially among the *assalariados*. Consequently, the services provided by the rural *sindicatos* must be maintained without interruption.

The alert regarding the advancement of COVID-19 occurred at the federation and territorial levels, through the various workers' union media (union journals, radio, social networks, e-mail), and sought to raise awareness about the contagion. Additionally, with the extinction of the Ministry of Labor, complaint and intervention by the auditors of the Ministry of Economy became even more complicated and difficult. Thus, rural workers have continued their activities in the fazendas, as usual. There are not many options to safeguard workers' health. However, Fetar has promoted the creation of a state crisis committee on the advancement of the COVID-19 pandemic in Rio Grande do Sul.

> In the city of Vacaria, as well as in the state of Rio Grande do Sul, we took all the precautions. Most Fetar-affiliated unions closed from March 19 to April 16 [2020]. Then they returned to service in Bagé, Uruguaiana, etc. We can't close the doors. There is medical care, dental care. We are open, at the moment. Employees of the federation [Fetar] are working from home. By phone, by computer. Our team [at Fetar] is always attentive. And the Fetag-affiliated unions too: our newspapers, radios, e-mail, everything remains the same [...] the coronavirus awareness campaign, preventions, what to do in the orchard [...]. Everything about the fight against

coronavirus. Fetar organized a state crisis committee. This committee was created by Fetar [...] together with the Ministry of Economy, Agapome, the legal adviser of Farsul, and others. What is the committee for? This committee was set up and it discussed how workplaces have to be maintained. On the farms, in packing, in rural area industry. We got the H1N1 vaccine [...] through the committee. We sent letters to those municipalities with more than a thousand rural employees (there are 18 municipalities in the state), and some replied. This would ease the H1N1 flu problem. We haven't had much return [...] When we receive complaints from the workers, immediately, public authorities are asked to supervise. Fetar is tracking the situation. At the moment, contamination is under control. Agriculture is not the food industry. We talked to the entrepreneurs, to Farsul, to the larger companies. There is monitoring. This committee dialogues [...]. (Fetar 1, Porto Alegre)

Workers know about the risk, but they don't always realize it. For example, when someone arrives from outside the property, for example, someone who comes from the city [...] they don't protect themselves! They do not take the necessary precautions. They talk, without wearing the mask, without keeping distance. (STR 2, Santana do Livramento)

According to what was reported by the interviewees, informality has also increased during the COVID-19 pandemic.

It is quite recurrent... There are several cases of workers without labor books. The *assalariado* says: 'My employer didn't sign the labor book. He doesn't want to sign it'. The worker was there [on the farm] for two months, working, and the employer did not want to sign the labor book. What do we do? The boss is not worrying about the admission test because of COVID-19. He says to the worker: 'There's no way, you can't go in town and take the exam because of COVID-19 [...] it is dangerous'. It's just an excuse not to sign the labor book. (STR, Alegrete)

In interviews conducted in July 2020, union leaders explained that there were no significant changes in the contractual clauses referring to the COVID-19 pandemic. As suggested, "it is always difficult to negotiate with the employer, even more now, in these times of coronavirus" (STR, Bagé). Work routines in rural areas were not modified in response to the coronavirus crisis: greater care is taken in bus transportation to the workplace, but little has changed in the organization of work.

> What changes with the pandemic? In practice, nothing changes. Work continues, generally in the open air. The risks are there, but nothing can be stopped. (STR, Alegrete)

During the pandemic, the participation of workers in assemblies has been increasingly reduced.

> Once we used to organize workers' meetings or assemblies in person, now we don't do it anymore. (STR, Mostardas)

> Because of coronavirus it is even more difficult to organize an assembly [...] it was even difficult before. (STR, Uruguaiana)

If collective bargaining doesn't change in order to respond to an emergency such as the coronavirus pandemic and the agreements by companies are very rare, what remains to be done is to approve a document and send it to the unions, companies and municipalities, to raise awareness about health prevention devices and other general guidelines. Fetar approved a *cartilha* (guidebook) in July 2020 and distributed it. The *cartilha* deals with various topics: creating and disclosing protocols for identifying and forwarding workers suspected of being contaminated by COVID-19 before entering the workplace, prevention of coronavirus infection, the correct form of hand hygiene and other prevention measures. It provides mechanisms and procedures for workers to report to employers if they are sick or have experienced symptoms; it restricts access to rural properties to those strictly necessary and provides best practices for workers belonging to a risk group. And yet, "there is no way to know how much the *cartilha* has been applied or not; employers don't even let us enter the fazendas" (Fetar 2, Porto Alegre).

The Puzzle of Representation

Rural workers' unions operate in a very complex and dynamic context, especially after the 2015 Ministerial Note no. 88, which permitted the workers' union to choose between a double (i.e., the so-called *sindicato eclético*) and a single professional category of representation. When I interviewed the presidents of an STAF, I always repeated the same question: *You became an STAF but you keep maintaining the same union charter, like when you were initially authorized to represent rural workers and family farmers* [...] *May I ask you, why don't you change your union charter?* In fact, an STR modifies its statute to become an STAF without modifying the union charter (which continues allowing double representation). Sometimes, the interviewees answered me like this: "I really don't know", "a good question", "we didn't realize", and so on. In other cases, the interviewee did not answer my question.

Thus, a *sindicato* can be engaged and achieve a good collective agreement (or not), develop grassroots union activity (or not), maintain *assalariados*' representation (or not) and provide health care services to rural workers (or not). On the one hand, some of the Fetag-affiliated workers' unions cooperated with Fetar and maintained the representation of *assalariados*; on the other hand, other Fetag-affiliated unions preferred to exclude double representation. There are still other differences among rural workers' unions. In Fetag-affiliated unions, for example, there is a group of 30 *sindicatos* questioning the Fetag: this group claims an excessive relegation on *assalariado* representation and an overly benevolent support to the state and federal governments.

Other differences are also encountered in relation to the party system. Politics is important and the agricultural sector has a huge influence. With regard to political representation, in 2020, 1037 farmers—among producers, landowners and agricultural professionals in general, but not wage earners—were elected to the municipalities of Rio Grande do Sul (among mayors and municipal councilors): a reduction compared to 2016, when there were 1178 (SEPLAG, 2021).

> In my opinion, unions and politics should be distinct. They shouldn't mix, but that's not the case [...] Two ex-presidents of Fetag, for example, Heitor Schuch and Elton Weber [...] the first is a federal deputy and the second is a state deputy. (STAF, Canguçu)

> Of course, there are political differences in Fetag [...] as well as in Fetar, even if they are smaller. I'm talking about leadership. There are the independent ones, those who support Bolsonaro, those who are left-oriented. Lots of differences. We have a lot of acquaintances, many contacts, many associate members [...] it is a political capital and some unions leaders run for municipal or state elections. There are also many political appointment positions. State and city government invited me to run elections [...] they offered me to hold political appointments, but I've always said no. I want to finish my term and retire. [...] Employers' unions are more aligned with

Bolsonaro. [...] when you enter the union premises you do not find political posters or party propaganda, but politics is around us. (STR, XXX)

Over time, family farming has become more autonomous and entrepreneurial, interested in achieving economic results. Family farming is increasingly distant from the communion of intentions that formerly united *assalariados* and family farming in a unique federation. A family farmer of Gaurama (in the northern region) describes the relations between a family farmer and a rural worker.

> Before, we were more like 'community'. There were fewer differences between owner and rural worker. I think about my father. After his death, his farm was divided equally among the children, but also considering the *assalariado*, who worked with him in the field [...] Today, many small farmers have grown and things, from this point of view, have changed. Small farmers have grown and are hiring employees. There is no longer that relationship, like with my father and the worker. Now it is different. The worker is no longer part of the family. He is an employee. (Family farmer, Gaurama)

A union leader of an STR in the Serra region spoke with me about his Fetag-affiliated *sindicato* and other Fetag-affiliated unions in the neighboring municipalities.

> Our farmer here is 'small', but he thinks as a 'large rural producer'. If he can take an *assalariado* and exploit him... he exploits him! And now... We are a rural workers' union. We are not Farsul. Farsul is connected to the CNA (Confederação Nacional de Agricultura) [National Confederation of Agriculture] of Brasilia. We don't. It is another professional category. If our small farmer, union member... thinks as an *estancieiro*... he might go with the other *estancieiros*, at Farsul. We have changed our statute. Because of Fetag. Fetag arrived here and said: 'you have to change the statutory regulation, it's a legal matter, they will create legal problems for you'. I would like to go back in time and keep the old statute. I would. But at every assembly, Fetag tells us to change the statute and become an STAF, at every meeting, at every regional assembly of Fetag-affiliated unions... they say that we must change: 'you have to get out of the *assalariados*' representation', 'there is no alternative'. We are the third largest union in the state. We have the *assalariados*, here in our territory. We have industries in the region, big industries with rural workers [...] the same problem all over the state [...] We should offer services [...] We represent and help the small farmer, but we want to sign a collective agreement. We asked our *ruralistas*' union, but they didn't

answer. We had a collective agreement. In previous years we had one. The employer union has an extension in our municipality, but this *sindicato ruralista*, which is based in Caxias do Sul, doesn't want to sign the agreement. […] I don't understand this tendency to get out of double representation. If there are employees in your territory, you must represent them. (STR, XXX)

However, dual union representation (*sindicalismo eclético*) is often frowned upon in interviews.

This 'eclectism' doesn't work. Employers say: 'In Venâncio Aires the salary is high. Workers have the unhealthy clause in the agreement... it's too much'. 'And when production is bad?' Here, come on, we have 80% informality. The people who grow tobacco, the *peão*... there is no law. It's just informal. They work two or three days a week: BRL 100 per day. Is a law missing? Or a real collective agreement that considers it all? There is no law for the day laborer. The *assalariado* himself doesn't care. In the assembly, when the new agreement is decided, no one goes. Rural worker comes to the union only if he is injured. The *assalariado* must participate. And there are worse situations than ours... in the municipalities around here. The *assalariado* works on a small property whose owner is a member of our union: how do we manage to represent both of them? I understand both sides, but there are a lot of eclectic unions that can't wait anymore to become an STAF. (STR, Venâncio Aires)

We have no interest in salaried employees. They are very few. (STR, Antônio Prado)

In Santa Cruz, the issue has been faced and resolved since 2014. In fact, our idea is the following: no longer representing the *assalariados* and signing another collective agreement representing family farmers. And Fetar, obviously, representing the *assalariados*. Two agreements: Fetar-*assalariados* with large producers and Fetar-*assalariados* with the STAFs representing family farmers. Who knows […] It is also a legal issue I would like to understand. (STR, Santa Cruz do Sul)

We have never represented them [the *assalariados*]. I don't understand why Farsul and Fetag are still divided. These structures were created in the past. Times change but we continue like that. (STR, Caxias do Sul)

> There are many cases that we cannot control. Among others, take for example the city of Porto Alegre. There are more than a thousand *assalariados* in the rural area of Porto Alegre. There is no collective agreement. Once there was also a *sindicato*. Today the union no longer works. It is simply closed. And what can we do? Almost nothing. We are the federation [Fetar], not the workers' union. (Fetar 2, Porto Alegre)

Canguçu is a municipality in the southern region of Rio Grande do Sul, considered the municipality with the largest number of small holdings in Brazil. With about 14,000 rural properties, it is recognized as the national capital of family agriculture. The STR was founded in the 1960s, received a *carta sindical* and represented the *assalariados* until a few years ago, when it decided to change the statute and move from being an STR to an STAF. Previously, care services were for everyone, but now they are only for family farmers. Moreover, CAGED registers the presence of over a thousand *assalariados* in the municipality.

> We have never signed a collective agreement. [...] An *assalariado* can join the union, but he must have an agricultural property and be a family farmer to receive assistance. (STR, Canguçu)

The growing differences between rural salaried workers and small farmers have also attracted the attention of Farsul-affiliated *sindicatos ruralistas* who now compete with Fetag unions to associate family farmers: more and more frequently, small farmers become members of the local *sindicato ruralista* (and therefore Farsul-affiliated) instead of the local STR or STAF, which are Fetag-affiliated unions.

> Here we compete for family farming. The *sindicato ruralista* thinks it is a kind of 'market'. *Ruralistas* compete with us because of the family farmers. The want to increase the number of memberships. (STR, Venâncio Aires)

> Today, actually. The family farmer as well as the small owner are disputed by the employers' unions and Fetag. In fact, the sooner STRs become STAFs, the better for us. (STR, Santa Cruz do Sul)

> Money is important and unions need money to survive. The more you associate family farmers, the more the economic income you receive. (STR, XXX)

Also, especially in the northern regions, another trend can be observed: other associations, instead of unions, have been created. These local associations are not trade unions. They do not hold a union charter but they do provide services. Family farmers expressed doubt about whether to choose to join these (new) associations or the local rural union.

> In our association, we have many family farmers who are not members of the local STR. If the local STR doesn't work well, we must help local family farmers. After all, the farmer himself chooses what to do, which association or *sindicato* to join in. We offer a lot of services, indeed. (Atraf, Antônio Prado)

The president of the STAF in Canguçu who commented on this litigation between STAFs and *sindicato ruralistas* shared a phrase that has stuck with me:

> After all, there is trade union freedom, and therefore a family farmer can register wherever he wants. (STR, Canguçu)

This idea of trade union freedom is generic and fundamentally erroneous. First of all, the problem of trade union freedom in Brazil is not the possibility of choosing between two employers' unions but rather the "single unionism" issue: only one union is the holder of the employee's representation and can sign the collective agreement. The worker can therefore join only one trade union, as there is only one representative trade union. Second, in Canguçu the STAF is the legal holder of the *assalariados*' representation, having not changed the union charter. Therefore, while the family farmer chooses between *sindicato ruralista* and STAF which, in both cases, will never sign a collective agreement, the rural worker does not have a union to represent him and never will: the right for his representation remains in the hands of the ex-STR of Canguçu, which is today an STAF. Third, it is evident that there is a problem of trade union freedom: in this case, in a municipality with more than a thousand *assalariados*, a collective agreement has never been signed. It is unlikely that a collective agreement will be concluded in Canguçu.

However, what is clear from the interviews is that the debate on union representation or on real union actions is not collective: each union follows its own internal logic, and the logic behind union policies must be analyzed at the level of the local union organization. The majority of Fetar unions are in the Pampa region, mainly because there are more *assalariados* in this region. As always, there are some exceptions: the president of the union of Alegrete, a city with a large extension of land in the middle of the Campanha, prefers to maintain its Fetag affiliation.

> Here, in our *sindicato*, we want to stay as we are, Fetag-affiliated, and we continue to represent the two categories: rural salaried workers and small farmers. We collaborate with Fetar. We have many *assalariados* here. (STR, Alegrete)

In addition to these internal differences within one's own state trade union system, it must also be considered that this puzzle is complicated by actors who are apparently external to the system of labor relations. It is also the case that other decisive actors enter the middle of these dynamics, complicating the scenario even more. In one particularly long interview, a union leader explained the role of accounting consultants to me and how this affects the union fund system, that is, the collection of the confederative contribution clause.

> Here we have a collective agreement. Every year we sign it. I don't know how many salaried workers we have. We have Caged data. But it is not very important. There are informal workers. [...] The employers send the employee to their accounting consultants. I know there are employees, but I don't know how many and where they are working. I don't know which accounting office assists these employees. We have employees with a formal contract. I don't know how many are working and what company they are working for. Offices do the payroll for landowners who have rural wage earners. [...] In our *convenção* we have a confederative contribution: it's a contractual clause. It's the law. There are offices that retain this confederative contribution, established in the collective agreement, and transfer it to the unions and other offices that don't retain this contribution. This contribution is important for Fetar to survive. For the unions to work. [...] There is another problem: dismissal is no longer approved here at the union, but at the accounting office. Sometimes we ratify. Just sometimes. There may even be a clause in the collective agreement, as there is, but the offices themselves advise the employer not to conduct dismissal at the union. We cannot control these accounting offices, which are allies of the *patrão*. Indeed, it is the *patrão* that pays them. Something similar happens almost everywhere in Rio Grande do Sul. (STR, XXX)

In practice, accounting consultants are important actors in the labor relations system: they condition union funding and are not independent actors but allies of the employers—"the employer who pays them" (STR, XXX).

> There's a very big office [of accounting consultants] here. They don't collect the confederative contribution. There is no way to report it. The office acts according to the interests of the boss and the boss speaks on behalf of the employee. By the way, the employee doesn't even go to the union. The employee doesn't even know where the union is. We don't even know where the accounting consultant is: each farm or company has its own labor consultant… but which? I don't know. There are a few workers who come here and we talk with them, also about the confederative contribution and others worker's rights. And the employee says: 'The boss told me I don't need to talk with the workers' union'. So, I explain. I invite them to speak with his colleagues. I inform them that we, at the STR, offer benefits for them: dentist, doctor. He doesn't pay anything else. But the accounting consultants and the boss say the worker doesn't need these things. The offices [of accounting consultants] don't show us anything. They say there are no longer employees: but in the Caged register there are a lot. Perhaps it is even true that they were reduced, but partially. They always answer the same way. What's going on? The dismissals are no longer carried out on union premises and union funding is reducing a lot. (STR, XXX)

To some extent, these dynamics occur almost everywhere in Rio Grande do Sul. In this context, "unionism is almost impossible […] without resources and with all these difficulties you can't unionize" (Fetar 2, Porto Alegre).

A Comparison

A typical issue in comparative political economy is the liaison between industrial relations systems and forms of capitalism. These hypotheses are generally developed in comparative schemes, more or less complex, to explain the performance of one system in comparison to the other. Of course, the present research does not conduct a comparative analysis, but it is interesting to consider the fact that, arriving in Santo Tomé, in the Argentinian province of Corrientes, via São Borja (Brazil), the system of labor relations profoundly changes. The province of Corrientes and São Borja are similar in terms of their habits and territorial identity, that is, the Pampa, with its long-held traditions and customs. However, in the province of Corrientes, the salary of a *peon peão* exceeds ARS 40,000 (around

BRL 2134.99), while in the municipalities of the Brazilian *pampa* the salary is around BRL 1300.

The Argentinian union has a complex structure, organized at various levels and strictly regulated by labor legislation: the hard core of the legislation maintains its legal basis from 1853 but the legislation was substantially reformed in 1994, including the protection of labor rights, through the insertion of article 14 bis. In Argentinian labor legislation, there is also a specific provision that regulates union associations: that is, Law 23.551 (Ley de Asociaciones Sindicales) approved in 1988. Law 23.551 contains a series of rights and duties pertaining to unions and provides for collective bargaining, strikes and other measures for union mobilization in its article 5. It is also important to remember that social dialogue and bargaining takes place at the National Tripartite Commission, composed by the state—when called upon by the parties—employers and employees. This centralized model of social dialogue presents significant differences from the Brazilian one.

Social dialogue in Argentina acts as an instrument of reconciliation among unions. In fact, the Comisión Nacional de Trabajo Agrario (a ministerial commission by Law 26.727/11 on *Trabajo Agrícola*) has already re-established the minimum working conditions of salary workers, as well as the provision of accommodation for rural workers. The main differences in the Brazilian case are therefore the centralization of bargaining (centrality is low in Brazil and high in Argentina because of national collective bargaining) and a different legal system that reduces uncertainties.

Moreover, in Argentina, rural unionism has its own distinct facets compared to other economic sectors. And in any case, the unitary worker representation is maintained. In the province of Corrientes there is no representation within the companies (farms) via union delegates. There are no local unions, but there are delegations of Uatre (Unión Argentina de Trabajadores Rurales y Estibadores) and the presence of the *obra social* Osprera (Obra Social del Personal Rural y Estibadores de la República Argentina). Also, Uatre is affiliated to union central CGT (Confederación General del Trabajo de la República Argentina) (Pontoni, 2016). In short, the Argentinian system is less fragmented.

Welfare is a central issue in both Brazil and Argentina. Workers' unions in Rio Grande do Sul provide services when public welfare doesn't guarantee them. The Argentine system guarantees the worker access to the provision of assistance services through the so-called *obras sociales*.

> Health provision for rural workers is organized by Osprera, which is controlled by Uatre: Osprera is part of Uatre. Uatre's Secretary General, José Voytenco, is also President of Osprera. Uatre is organized like a pyramid. Centralized in Buenos Aires, but we have a delegation within the province. Always Uatre's delegation. Here, we only have Uatre and a provincial delegate. But it is very difficult to relate with rural workers. Currently, we have 25 departments! Uatre has its headquarters in Corrientes. In the province of Corrientes today, we have 30,000 workers affiliated with Uatre. Not everyone is in our *obra social*. Someone is with another *obra*. There are other *obras sociales* with greater coverage but the workers continue to still be affiliated with Uatre. Only a minority, 10%, of members are not in Osprera […] In Argentina, the collective agreement is linked to activity in the region. It is discussed in each zone. In the same province, the provincial delegate makes this discussion with the employers, with the mediation of the national state as well. Three actors: Uatre, government, employers. Forestry, citrus, *yerba mate*, horticulture, floriculture. When we analyze the salary, it is linked to the activity of each city. That is… within the same contract there are different activities. (Employee Osprera, Corrientes)

Uatre has a delegate for the entire province. The same structure organized at the provincial level is reproduced at the local level. The local secretary reports to the provincial delegate, who is the top Uatre delegate for each province. Above the provincial delegate is a national delegate, and all provincial delegates report to the general secretary.

> […] there are many complaints. Last year, there were workers in sub-human conditions, sleeping on the floor. Abandoned people. In appalling conditions, but there were complaints. Uatre and the Ministry of Labor… are part of these inspections Also, these are the words of the secretary general… there are still 500,000 in Argentina. It's very difficult to get to that person too. That worker. There goes the police force, the national gendarmerie. Strikes we don't have. There is no strike. Those who live in the countryside are not informed. Country life is difficult. (Employee Osprera, Corrientes)

In terms of collective labor rights, Argentina has ratified the International Labour Organization (ILO) convention on freedom of association (No. 87), while Brazil has not yet ratified it. In addition to union freedom (in other words, "single unionism"), there are other differences. The welfare system, for example, is mirrored in Argentine labor relations (*obra sociales*). Argentine unionism configures itself as a model that can undergo reforms without changing the configuration and function of the model itself: it has a high degree of centralization, with maintenance of the tripartite system and union financing by affiliation and *obra sociales*.

Territorial bargaining among local *sindicatos* in Rio Grande do Sul does not guarantee significant advances in terms of salaries: many small unions with very similar agreements are marked by territorialization that divides the workforce. In a context like that of Pampa—with no strikes and a union culture that is stubbornly opposed to conflict and strikes—only a centralized system can guarantee the representation of work and significant advances in terms of wages. The only element that the Argentinian and Brazilian unions have in common, unfortunately, is the system of informality at work.

References

Pontoni, G. A. (2016). Capacidad de negociación colectiva en Argentina, 1991–2011: La experiencia reciente del gremio camionero. *Revista de Ciências sociais, 29*(39), 131–154.

SEPLAG. (2021). Desigualdades de gênero dos ocupados com atividades ligadas à agricultura no RS. *Relatório Técnico*. Governo do Estado do Rio Grande do Sul. Departamento de Economia e Estatística. Retrieved November 17, 2021, from https://www.estado.rs.gov.br/estudo-do-dee-spgg-aponta-desigualdade-de-genero-nas-atividades-ligadas-ao-campo-no-rs?fbclid=IwAR1aqHnqs16M0vnr0Kdh_4wsZroHd7SS9M-hRXTpcT_ekLsDTL5riHxRlok

CHAPTER 5

Final Considerations

Abstract The case of Rio Grande do Sul is not an isolated one. In this chapter, institutional pressures from the federal government and economic lobbies are discussed.

Keywords Labor representation • Brazilian party system • Political lobbying

There Is an Elephant in the Room

In December 2016, President Michel Temer supported the approval of a constitutional amendment that retained spending on health care, education and public investments for 20 years (EC 95). In 2017, two important laws were passed (Laws 13.429 and 13.467) amending the laws related to temporary work (Law 6.019/1974) and the Consolidation of Labor Law (CLT). With the arrival of Jair Bolsonaro, the neo-liberal agenda of Temer's government was strengthened. The first act of the newly elected president was the dissolution of the country's Ministry of Labor on January 1, 2019 (MP 870/2019). The MP has had practical effects: for example, compliance with security measures in private companies through labor inspectors would now be managed directly by the Ministry of Economy.

In 2019, the so-called Economic Freedom Law (Law 13.874) promoted further amendments to the CLT. Another constitutional amendment (EC 103) profoundly changed the social security system. Finally, several provisional measures enacted in 2020 amended labor relation regulations, one of which has already been passed into law (Law 14.020). All of these amendments and changes have had an effect on both material law and labor procedural law. Moreover, during the COVID-19 pandemic, the federal government adopted other legal measures to encourage the dismissal of employees and obstruct the union (MP 927/2020 and MP 936/2020).

The labor reform didn't improve Brazilian employment statistics. Rogério Marinho, the deputy rapporteur of the labor reform proposal, stated that intermittent work would achieve extraordinary results: "millions of Brazilians who are now unemployed, underemployed or who have given up looking for a job, after years of fruitless searching, will be integrated into the labor market" (Agência Câmara de Notícias, 2015). However, the (obvious) result has been different: transforming minimally stable labor agreements into intermittent labor agreements didn't result in an increase in terms of job posts but led to even more job precariousness. The labor market reached a rather embarrassing level of unemployment: the average unemployment rate for the year 2020 was 13.5%, the highest since 2012 (with about 13.4 million people waiting for a job). The result for the year 2020 interrupted the fall in unemployment that began in 2018, when it was 12.3%. In 2019, unemployment was 11.9%. Also, the informality rate rose from 41.1% in 2019 to 38.7% in 2020, which represented 33.3 million people without a formal contract (employees in the private sector or domestic workers) (IBGE, 2021).

During the coronavirus pandemic, the program for the temporary reduction of wages and suspension of employment contracts (MP 936) helped to preserve 11,698,243 jobs. According to Agência Brasil (Máximo, 2020) the amounts to be paid for supplementary income rose to R$17.4 billion. Significant social segments were clearly limiting their basic expenses with food and clothing when they were not taking out bank loans so that they could cover their regular and basic expenses (Gandra, 2020). In addition, about 64% of collective bargaining renewed in May 2021 had results below inflation (Dieese, 2020, 2021). The Brazilian scenario is marked by material deprivation and extreme inequality: over one-third of the population has no internet access; 31.1 million people have no access to running water; 74.2 million people (37% of the Brazilian population) live in areas without sewage treatment and 5.8 million families do not have a bathroom at home (Brasil Econômico, 2020).

Poverty and inequality have increased at the same time: the 2019 continuous Pesquisa Nacional por Amostra de Domicílios [National Household Sample Survey] (PNAD) study indicates that the income of the 1% of the people who earn more in Brazil is equivalent to 33.7 times the income of half the population who earn less. While the average monthly income of those who earn more from work is BRL 28,659, the average income of those of those who earn less is BRL 850 (Saraiva & Peret, 2019; Estatísticas sociais, 2019, 2020). If it was possible to finance the loss of work during the pandemic, it was only thanks to Congress and to increases in emergency aid payments initially proposed by the government for self-employed workers, which rose from BRL 200 to BRL 600 (Mazon, 2020). Meanwhile, the net profits of financial institutions in Brazil in 2018 were the most expressive since 1994, amounting to BRL 98.5 billion, second only to 2019. From July 2018 to June 2019, banks made profits amounting to BRL 109 billion, according to the Brazilian Central Bank's inspection director. The growth in net profits in 2019 was 18%, and four institutions alone accumulated profits amounting to BRL 81.5 billion (G1, 2019).

In addition to this planned inequality, a development model that is anything but virtuous is added: the latifundium. The first allegations of slave labor revealed by the Comissão Pastoral da Terra (CPT) date back to the early 1970s—like the CPT itself. The systematic computation of information on this crime is gradually consolidated from 1985 onwards. From 1995, when the first rescues of enslaved workers through the Special Mobile Inspection Groups began, until 2018, 50,106 thousand workers were freed from slave labor conditions across the country. A study by the NGO Reporter Brasil, prepared in 2004, followed the supply chain of those 96 farms reported on the dirty list (*lista suja*) of the Ministry of Labor at the time. These fazendas supplied beef, sugar cane, coffee, charcoal, soy, cotton and black pepper to domestic and foreign companies, some of them among the largest in the country (Plassat, 2015). Of the total of 35,943 slave workers rescued in Brazil between 2003 and 2018, the majority are men (95%). Most are between 30 and 39 years old. While 33% are illiterate, another 40% attended only elementary school; 41% are *pardos* (i.e., having grayish-brown skin), 24% white, 12% black, 19% East Asians and 4% indigenous persons (Repórter Brasil, 2020).

Slave labor is expressly prohibited by article 149 of the penal code, but fighting against it is not automatic: financial resources are needed. The government of Bolsonaro has drastically reduced the amount allocated to fight slave labor in the country. The resources, which have been shrinking year after year, are used to purchase fuel, daily rates, airline tickets and other expenses to carry out rescue operations. In 2020, BRL 1.3 million was spent on fighting slave labor, a reduction of 41% compared to 2019, when BRL 2.3 million was spent, an amount that had already shrunk compared to 2018, when R$2.7 million in funds was allocated (Longo, 2021).

Constitutional Amendment (EC) 81 of 2014, which punishes rural properties that practice slave labor with expropriation, was enacted by the National Congress in 2021. Yet it still requires regulation through a complementary law that defines what would be considered slave labor (G1, 2021). On May 1, 2021, during his participation in the opening ceremony of the 86th edition of ExpoZebu, President Bolsonaro said that EC 81 would not be regulated in his government. According to the president, the amendment should be revised.

A strong political base and an institutionalized lobbying system are needed for enacting these policies. The Bancada Ruralista (i.e., the Parliamentary Agricultural Front), is one of the largest and most active benches in the Chamber of Deputies, made up of more than 200 federal deputies (out of a total of 513) from various parties. It defends public policies to encourage agribusiness. In general, the *Bancada* demands the expansion of rural financing and the flexibilization of labor legislation and criticizes environmental legislation. For rural landowners, the demarcation of indigenous lands (i.e., the so-called APA, *Àreas de Proteção Ambiental* [Environmental Protection Areas]) represents an obstacle to the advancement of agribusiness. The *Bancada* played a decisive role in the approval of the Brazilian Forest Code in 2012. Under the influence of rural producers, the new legislation gave amnesty to producers who deforested, until July 2008, above what was permitted and determined by the previous law. The *ruralista* caucus was also decisive in the approval by Congress of a Provisional Measure (MP) in June 2017, which changed the federal government's land distribution policy.

The Crisis of Labor Representation

Workers' unions in Rio Grande do Sul are sub-divided between hundreds of local unions, three federations and two central unions with different levels of affiliations within the party system. On the contrary, the *sindicatos ruralistas* are unitarily Farsul-affiliated, without any divisions, and with powerful political representatives at both the federal and state levels. Only 26% of municipalities are covered by a collective agreement. Labor relationships include a major part of regularly hired workers but exclude part of the legally hired workers as well as all of the informal workers. Additionally, a significant and increasing number of Fetag-affiliated Sindicatos dos Trabalhadores Rurais (STRs) are ready to leave the double system of representation (i.e., the *sindicato eclético*) to dedicate themselves solely to family farming. Meanwhile, a political agenda made up of support for agrobusiness, anti-environmentalism and anti-union policy advances across the country. In my view, the enormous territory that surrounds the streets of Rio Grande do Sul's cities, financed by large landowners who praise President Bolsonaro represent a junction between the macro-system described above and my micro-level analysis. Support for Bolsonaro, both moral and political, is widespread in the trade unions (especially in Farsul and a little less in Fetag) and among workers.

Respondents suggest some tools and strategies to improve collective bargaining and working conditions: a centralized collective agreement (at the state level, with greater coverage), the creation of regional wage-earners' unions representing solely the *assalariados*, the promotion of a consistent social dialogue, a consortium of companies to legally hire rural workers (using an economy of scale to reduce labor costs), a clearer and more transparent system of representation and union financing. However, it is precisely because of this macro- and micro-system that the political conditions for a better job are still missing.

The labor relation system is going through a crisis, indeed. According to Pierson (1998), it is possible to attribute four meanings to the notion of crisis: (1) a situation of disturbance caused by an external shock, (2) a manifestation of a long-term contradiction, (3) a dramatic moment that precedes the overcoming of a situation, and (4) any large-scale and lasting problem.

The arrival of Temer and then Bolsonaro to the government represents a shock for the trade union movement (1). Bolsonaro is clear: "The unions are the ones that most hinder Brazil" (Estadão Conteúdo, 2019). I suppose he is not referring to the Farsul-affiliated unions. The victory of Bolsonaro in the presidential election was celebrated by Farsul: it represented a new direction, aligned with the thinking of the Brazilian agrobusiness community. Yet at least Farsul has been ideologically coherent, while the Fetag has been far more ambiguous.

The 2017 labor reform surprised the workers' unions (Carbonai, 2018). In hindsight, given the changes introduced in 2017, Fetar probably wouldn't even have been born, remaining anchored to Fetag. The eclecticism of rural unionism, however, represents a historical contradiction, never clearly intervened upon (2). Also, the interviews I conducted reflect a growing common understanding between Farsul-affiliated and Fetag-affiliated unions. The elements of identity in common between family farming and agribusiness are increasing over time. As some interviewees say, rural employers, large or small, are always entrepreneurs. And they both hire the *assalariados* because of the same collective agreement. In addition, there are the various programs of SENAR (Serviço Nacional de Aprendizagem Rural) and other state government commissions in which both Fetag and Farsul participate: "there are more and more elements in common (cultural, economic, social, political) between small farming and Farsul" (Sindicato de Trabalhadores da Agricultura Familiar (STAF), Caxias do Sul).

Scholars have identified the development of collective identities, the mobilization of external expertise and the development of union leadership as key resources in the union renewal process (Croucher & Wood, 2017; Levesque & Murray, 2006). Who are the political activists in Rio Grande do Sul who can now revitalize trade unions and solve the precariousness of rural work? Unfortunately, this group is limited: Fetar-affiliated unions and a reduced number of Fetag-affiliated unions in dispute with the policies of the federation. As always, institutional pressures push up against the union representation of rural workers.

The number of slave workers, very high informality, the numbers of occupational accidents, wage levels, the difficulties that occur during collective bargaining, and the use of pesticides outline the contours of a dramatic moment (3). Moreover, a plan to overcome the difficulties of this moment has not yet been outlined, while executable proposals for a new a model of labor relations appear to exist as a countertrend.

For the moment, PEC 196/2019 is advancing in Congress: PEC 196 is an amendment to the Federal Constitution that could modify the entire Brazilian industrial relations system, aiming for adhesion to ILO's

Convention no. 87 (Freedom of Association and Protection of the Right to Organize). However, it is unlikely that PEC 196/2019 will be approved. Furthermore, a constitutional amendment is not useful without a serious debate about (state and national) social dialogue. In any case, it is necessary to find a model of worker union representation that guarantees greater achievements. This much is evident.

Still, there is ample room for maneuver and initiative. For example, the informal labor market could be reduced by a consortium of employers or by a group of small business owners who decide to hire a farm worker. Instead of informality, the laborer could work regularly for a larger company (the consortium), which guarantees his or her labor rights. There are other proposals as well. As interviewees suggest, because of a state-centered system of bargaining (i.e., a unique collective agreement at the state level or a reduced number of regional agreement) coverage would increase and informality would be reduced, guaranteeing more substantial gains. As usual, "it takes two to tango". Additionally, new rural workers' unions could be created, at the regional level, representing the *assalariados* for whom representation is not guaranteed by Fetag-affiliated unions nor by Fetraf-affiliated unions (e.g., in Antônio Prado and Santa Cruz do Sul). It is also fundamental to favor the control and tracing of agricultural products in the supply chain through a certification system that allows us to understand not only the quality of the product but also the quality of the work.

So too a feeling of class identity must be built, as well as a union identity. Is the rural *sindicato* a service union? Some unions provide medical assistance, others don't. Rural unionism is complex and ambiguous, indeed. STAFs are increasing: the majority of STR members of Fetag are in the process of changing their statutes to stop representing the *assalariados*.

In addition to union representation, there is a large-scale and enduring problem of political representation within the agricultural sector (4). Eduardo Leite, the governor of Rio Grande do Sul, has chosen to legally release agro-toxins to satisfy his allied rural political base. PL 260/2020, which amends §2 of Art. 1 of State Law No. 7.747/82, "provides for the control of pesticides and other biocides at the state level". Also, the new state secretary of labor, employment and income of Rio Grande do Sul, Ronaldo Nogueira, formerly the minister of labor in the government of Temer, was the target, in 2019, of a censorship sanction by the National Council of Human Rights (CNDH). Censorship is the consequence of conduct contrary to human rights: Nogueira obstructed the disclosure of the register of employers who submitted workers to conditions analogous to slave labor. If that wasn't enough, he also enacted Ordinance 1.129/2017, which was the target of a series of criticisms by human rights organizations due to the fact that it provided for a possible slowdown in the fight against slave labor. Ordinance 1.129/2017 changed the concept of slave labor and made inspection unfeasible. With the pretext of regulating the payment of unemployment insurance to workers rescued from slave labor and updating the *lista suja*, the ordinance reformulated the concept of contemporary slave labor and imposed a series of difficulties to impede inspection and the publication of the *lista suja*.

The largest lobby in Congress, the Bancada Ruralista, controls one-fourth of the house. The rural caucus in Congress is well represented by representatives from Rio Grande do Sul. In 2013, a speech by Luis Carlos Heinze (Partido Progressista, PP) ran on social networks, in which he defined *quilombolas*, Indians, gays and lesbians as "useless" and encouraged farmers to arm themselves against social movements. Its political intention was to defend agribusiness, expand the use of pesticides and, ultimately, enrich the rich. As the founder of the São Borja Rice Association, federal deputy Heinze wanted to change the rule that requires the printing of the transgenic symbol on products. He has already tried to exempt rice from the payment of Social Integration Programming (PIS) and Contribution to Social Security Financing (Confins) by increasing the rate for importers. During his period as a parliamentarian, Heinze's wealth has grown: in 2006, Heinze declared to the Superior Electoral Court (TSE) that he had BRL 1.6 million in goods. In 2018, the *ruralista* recorded BRL 8.3 million, an increase of 419% (Castilho, 2018).

As previously mentioned, *ruralistas* in Rio Grande do Sul are well represented in the national congress. One such *ruralista*, Alceu Moreira (Movimento Democrático Brasileiro), was quoted calling indigenous people *vigaristas* [professional fraudsters] and encouraged a militia to be mounted against them. The deputy was accused of receiving a bribe of R$200,000, according to a statement by Ricardo Saud, the director of JBS (a Brazilian meat processor operating worldwide and involved in a nationwide corruption scandal). Like Heinze, Moreira's patrimony has been growing. Between 2006 and 2018, Moreira's equity jumped 432%, from R$488,000 to R$2.6 million, according to a statement of the TSE. Another committed opponent of social movements among the *ruralistas* in Rio Grande do Sul is federal deputy Jerônimo Goergen (PP). In June 2016, he presented 29 legislative decrees suspending 826,600 hectares of rural areas for agrarian reform and the regularization of indigenous and *quilombola* territories. He is also the author of a project that classifies the Landless Rural Workers Movement (MST) and the Homeless Workers Movement (MTST) as terrorist groups. Like Alceu Moreira, Goergen was quoted by the JBS director Ricardo Saud in a statement to the federal police and had received a bribe of R$100,000 in September 2014. When he entered politics in 2006, Goergen declared that he had in his name a common car and a house, totaling R$211,000 in possessions. In 2018, his worth rose 516% in equity, ultimately reaching R$1.3 million in assets alone (Castilho, 2018).

In this scenario, labor is only partially represented. A new labor relation system with clear political representation is urgently needed to improve upon these imperfections, as are ongoing discussions oriented toward determining whether the current model works or whether it does not. Until then, what committed rural workers' unions in Rio Grande do Sul can do is limited to copying strategies, means of resisting the constant pressures and systemic difficulties, attempts to advance by distinguishing between risks and opportunities, and ongoing efforts to open up new spaces for lawful and dignified labor practice.

References

Agência Câmara de Notícias. (2015). Relator diz que reforma trabalhista vai gerar empregos; outros deputados contestam. https://www.camara.leg.br/noticias/509038-relator-diz-que-reforma-trabalhista-vai-gerar-empregos-outros-deputados-contestam

Brasil Econômico. (2020, March 28). Desafios: Brasil tem 31,3 milhões de pessoas sem água encanada e casas lotadas. Retrieved September 7, 2021, from https://economia.ig.com.br/2020-03-28/desafios-brasil-tem-313-milhoes-de-pessoas-sem-agua-encanada-e-casas-lotadas.html

Carbonai, D. (2018). Labour reform in Brazil, politics, and sindicatos: Notes on the general strikes of 2017. *Journal of Politics in Latin America, 11*(2), 231–245. https://doi.org/10.1177/1866802X19861493

Castilho, L. (2018, September 4). O agro é lobby: a bancada ruralista no congress. *Le monde diplomatique*. Retrieved September 19, 2019, from https://diplomatique.org.br/o-agro-e-lobby-a-bancada-ruralista-no-congresso/

Croucher, R., & Wood, G. (2017). Union renewal in historical perspective. *Work, Employment and Society, 31*(6), 1010–1020. https://doi.org/10.1177/0950017017713950

Dieese. (2020). Acordos negociados pelas entidades sindicais para enfrentar a pandemia do coronavírus. *Estudos e Pesquisas*, 91. https://www.dieese.org.br/estudosepesquisas/2020/estPesq92AcordosCovidAtualizacao.html

Dieese. (2021). *De olho nas negociações*. Reajustes salariais em maio de 2021. 9. https://www.dieese.org.br/boletimnegociacao/2021/boletimnegociacao09.pdf

Estadão Conteúdo. (2019, May 12). Sindicatos atrapalham país por legislarem em causa própria, diz Bolsonaro. Retrieved January 7, 2021, from https://exame.com/brasil/sindicatos-atrapalham-pais-por-legislarem-em-causa-propria-diz-bolsonaro/

Estatísticas Sociais. (2019, May 31). PNAD Contínua trimestral: desocupação cresce em 14 das 27 UFs no 1° trimestre de 2019. Agência IBGE. Retrieved January 7, 2021, from https://agenciadenoticias.ibge.gov.br/agencia-sala-de-imprensa/2013-agencia-de-noticias/releases/24486-pnad-continua-trimestral-desocupacao-cresce-em-14-das-27-ufs-no-1-trimestre-de-2019

Estatísticas sociais. (2020, May 31). PNAD Contínua 2019: rendimento do 1% que ganha mais equivale a 33,7 vezes o da metade da população que ganha menos. Retrieved January 7, 2021. https://agenciadenoticias.ibge.gov.br/agencia-sala-de-imprensa/2013-agencia-de-noticias/releases/27594-pnad-continua-2019-rendimento-do-1-que-ganha-mais-equivale-a-33-7-vezes-o-da-metade-da-populacao-que-ganha-menos

G1. (2019, March 11). Rentabilidade de bancos brasileiros é a maior em 7 anos e lucro bate recorde, revela BC. https://g1.globo.com/economia/noticia/2019/04/11/rentabilidade-de-bancos-brasileiros-e-a-maior-em-7-anos-revela-banco-central.ghtml

G1. (2021, January 5). Com participação de Bolsonaro e ministra da Agricultura, Expozebu 2021 é aberta oficialmente em Uberaba com formato virtual. https://g1.globo.com/mg/triangulo-mineiro/noticia/2021/05/01/com-participacao-de-bolsonaro-e-ministra-da-agricultura-expozebu-2021-e-aberta-oficialmente-em-uberaba-com-formato-virtual.ghtml

Gandra, A. (2020). Percentual de famílias com dívidas atinge recorde em março. Agência Brasil. *Agência Brasil*. Retrieved May 2020, from https://agenciabrasil.ebc.com.br/economia/noticia/2020-03/percentual-de-familias-com-dividas-atinge-recorde-em-marco

IBGE. (2021). Desemprego recua para 13,9% no 4° tri, mas taxa média do ano é a maior desde 2012. *Agência IBGE Notícias*. https://agenciadenoticias.ibge.gov.br/agencia-noticias/2012-agencia-de-noticias/noticias/30130-desemprego-recua-para-13-9-no-quarto-trimestre-mas-e-o-maior-para-o-ano-desde-2012

Levesque, C., & Murray, G. (2006). How do unions renew? Paths to union renewal. *Labour Studies Journal, 31*(3), 1–13. https://doi.org/10.1177/0160449X0603100301

Longo, I. (2021, February 21). Bolsonaro reduz verba para combate ao trabalho escravo em mais de 40%. *Revista forum.* https://revistaforum.com.br/direitos/bolsonaro-reduz-verba-para-combate-ao-trabalho-escravo-em-mais-de-40/

Máximo, W. (2020, June 26). *Programa de redução de salário preserva 11,7 milhões de empregos.* Agência Brasil. https://agenciabrasil.ebc.com.br/economia/noticia/2020-06/programa-de-reducao-de-salario-preserva-117-milhoes-de-empregos

Mazon, E. (2020, March 5). Cesta básica fica 13,89% mais cara em 12 meses. *Zero horas.* https://gauchazh.clicrbs.com.br/economia/dicas-de-economia/noticia/2020/03/cesta-basica-fica-1389-mais-cara-em-12-meses-ck7e0j4jr01ie01pqqxxllbwt.html

Pierson, P. (1998). *Beyond the welfare state. The new political economy of welfare.* Polity Press.

Plassat, X. (2015). Campanha nacional da CPT contra o trabalho escravo. https://www.cptnacional.org.br/publicacoes/noticias/trabalho-escravo/2634-cpt-30-anos-de-denuncia-e-combate-ao-trabalho-escravo

Repórter Brasil. (2020). Trabalho escravo e gênero: Quem são as trabalhadoras escravizadas no Brasil? In N. Suzuki (Ed.), *Escravo, nem pensar.* Repórter Brasil.

Saraiva, A., & Peret, E. (2019, March 30). Desemprego sobe para 12,7% com 13,4 milhões de pessoas em busca de trabalho. *Estatísticas Sociais.* Retrieved January 7, 2021. https://agenciadenoticias.ibge.gov.br/agencia-noticias/2012-agencia-de-noticias/noticias/24283-desemprego-sobe-para-12-7-com-13-4-milhoes-de-pessoas-em-busca-de-trabalho

References

Agência Câmara de Notícias. (2015). Relator diz que reforma trabalhista vai gerar empregos; outros deputados contestam. https://www.camara.leg.br/noticias/509038-relator-diz-que-reforma-trabalhista-vai-gerar-empregos-outros-deputados-contestam

Antonello, L. (2021, March 4). Dezoito trabalhadores são resgatados de trabalho escravo e tráfico de pessoas na Serra. *Zero Hora*. https://gauchazh.clicrbs.com.br/pioneiro/geral/noticia/2021/03/dezoito-trabalhadores-sao-resgatados-de-trabalho-escravo-e-trafico-de-pessoas-na-serra-cklvieef6003f016ubc3mrk55.html

Baccaro, L. (2008). Contrattazione politica e consultazione dei lavoratori. *Quaderni di Rassegna sindacale, 9*(1), 125–135.

Bandeira, P. S. (2003). Algumas Hipóteses sobre as Causas das Diferenças Regionais quanto ao Capital Social no Rio Grande do Sul. In S. M. Correa de Souza (Ed.), *Capital Social e Desenvolvimento Regional*. Edunisc.

Baquero, M., & Prá, J. R. (2007). *A democracia brasileira e a cultura política no Rio Grande do Sul*. UFRGS Editora.

Bell, S. (1999). *Campanha Gaúcha: A Brazilian ranching system, 1850–1920*. Stanford University Press.

Boito, A. (1991). *O sindicalismo de Estado no Brasil: uma análise crítica da estrutura sindical*. Editora da Unicamp.

Brasil Econômico. (2020, March 28). Desafios: Brasil tem 31,3 milhões de pessoas sem água encanada e casas lotadas. Retrieved September 7, 2021, from https://economia.ig.com.br/2020-03-28/desafios-brasil-tem-313-milhoes-de-pessoas-sem-agua-encanada-e-casas-lotadas.html

© The Author(s), under exclusive license to Springer Nature Switzerland AG 2022
D. Carbonai, *Rural Workers, Sindicatos and Collective Bargaining in Rio Grande do Sul*, https://doi.org/10.1007/978-3-030-94808-5

Brazil. (2014). Nota Técnica n. 88. In *Ministério do Trabalho e Emprego. Manual de Procedimentos de Registro Sindical*. MTE.

Carbonai, D. (2018). Labour reform in Brazil, politics, and sindicatos: Notes on the general strikes of 2017. *Journal of Politics in Latin America, 11*(2), 231–245. https://doi.org/10.1177/1866802X19861493

Carbonai, D., & Lentz J. R. L. (Host). (2020). *Sociologia do trabalho*. https://open.spotify.com/show/14Fqtgd2vP8y9PrHhyOcmA

Castilho, L. (2018, September 4). O agro é lobby: a bancada ruralista no congress. *Le monde diplomatique*. Retrieved September 19, 2019, from https://diplomatique.org.br/o-agro-e-lobby-a-bancada-ruralista-no-congresso/

Coletti, C. (1998). *A estrutura sindical no campo*. Unicamp.

Collins, R. (1985). *Three sociological traditions*. Oxford University.

Colombi, A. P. (2019). As Centrais Sindicais e a Reforma Trabalhista. Enfrentamentos e Dificuldades. *Tempo Social, 31*(3), 217–236. https://doi.org/10.11606/0103-2070.ts.2019.152129

Colvero, R. B., Paniagua, E. R., & Carbonai, D. (2014). Uruguaina: suas Fronteiras e sua Identidade. *Estudios históricos, 12*, 1–16. http://www.estudioshistoricos.org/12/artigo%20uruguaiana.pdf

Cook, M. L. (2007). *The politics of labour reform in Latin America: between flexibility and rights*. The Pennsylvania State University.

Cregan, C., Bartram, T., & Stanton, P. (2009). Union organizing as a mobilizing strategy: The impact of social identity and transformational leadership on the collectivism of union members. *British Journal of Industrial Relations, 47*(4), 701–722.

Croucher, R., & Wood, G. (2017). Union renewal in historical perspective. *Work, Employment and Society, 31*(6), 1010–1020. https://doi.org/10.1177/0950017017713950

Di Franco, G. (2006). *Corrispondenze multiple e altre tecniche multivariate per variabili categoriali*. Milan, FrancoAngeli.

Dieese. (2020). Acordos negociados pelas entidades sindicais para enfrentar a pandemia do coronavírus. *Estudos e Pesquisas*, 91. https://www.dieese.org.br/estudosepesquisas/2020/estPesq92AcordosCovidAtualizacao.html

Dieese. (2021). De olho nas negociações. Reajustes salariais em maio de 2021. 9. https://www.dieese.org.br/boletimnegociacao/2021/boletimnegociacao09.pdf

Estadão Conteúdo. (2019, May 12). Sindicatos atrapalham país por legislarem em causa própria, diz Bolsonaro. Retrieved January 7, 2021, from https://exame.com/brasil/sindicatos-atrapalham-pais-por-legislarem-em-causa-propria-diz-bolsonaro/

Estatísticas Sociais. (2019, May 31). PNAD Contínua trimestral: desocupação cresce em 14 das 27 UFs no 1° trimestre de 2019. Agência IBGE. Retrieved January 7, 2021, from https://agenciadenoticias.ibge.gov.br/agencia-sala-de-imprensa/2013-agencia-de-noticias/releases/24486-pnad-continua-trimestral-desocupacao-cresce-em-14-das-27-ufs-no-1-trimestre-de-2019

Estatísticas sociais. (2020, May 31). PNAD Contínua 2019: rendimento do 1% que ganha mais equivale a 33,7 vezes o da metade da população que ganha menos. Retrieved January 7, 2021. https://agenciadenoticias.ibge.gov.br/agencia-sala-de-imprensa/2013-agencia-de-noticias/releases/27594-pnad-continua-2019-rendimento-do-1-que-ganha-mais-equivale-a-33-7-vezes-o-da-metade-da-populacao-que-ganha-menos

Favareto, A. (2006). Agricultores, Trabalhadores: os Trinta Anos do Novo Sindicalismo Rural no Brasil. *Revista Brasileira de Ciências Sociais, 21*(62), 27–44. https://doi.org/10.1590/S0102-69092006000300002

Fehlberg, M. F., Santos, I. S., & Tomasi, E. (2001). Acidentes de trabalho na zona rural de Pelotas, Rio Grande do Sul, Brasil: um estudo transversal de base populacional. *Caderno de Saúde Pública, 17*(6), 1375–1381.

Ferreira de Siqueira, D., De Moura, R. M., Laurentino, G. C., Silva, G. F., Soares, L. D., & Lima, B. R. (2012). Qualidade de Vida de Trabalhadores Rurais e Agrotóxicos: uma Revisão Sistemática. *Revista Brasileira de Ciências da Saúde, 16*(2), 259–266. https://doi.org/10.4034/RBCS.2012.16.02.22

Fetar. (2019). Acidentes com Máquinas Agrícolas. Alterações nas Normas Regulamentadoras. In *IV Seminário de segurança e saúde do trabalhador rural*. Fetar.

Fiori, T. (2021). *Erradicação da pobreza: ODS 1 no Rio Grande do Sul*. Secretaria de Planejamento.

Frantz, T. R., & Silva Neto, B. (2015). A formação histórica dos sistemas agrários do Rio Grande do Sul. In B. S. Neto & D. Basso (Eds.), *Os sistemas agrários do Rio Grande do Sul: análise e recomendações de políticas* (pp. 33–98). Unijuí.

Freire, D. (2018, November 23). Em 'agonia', sindicatos demitem e vendem imóveis para sobrevive. *Veja*. https://veja.abril.com.br/economia/em-agonia-sindicatos-demitem-e-vendem-imoveis-para-sobreviver/

G1. (2019, March 11). Rentabilidade de bancos brasileiros é a maior em 7 anos e lucro bate recorde, revela BC. https://g1.globo.com/economia/noticia/2019/04/11/rentabilidade-de-bancos-brasileiros-e-a-maior-em-7-anos-revela-banco-central.ghtml

G1. (2021, January 5). Com participação de Bolsonaro e ministra da Agricultura, Expozebu 2021 é aberta oficialmente em Uberaba com formato virtual. https://g1.globo.com/mg/triangulo-mineiro/noticia/2021/05/01/com-participacao-de-bolsonaro-e-ministra-da-agricultura-expozebu-2021-e-aberta-oficialmente-em-uberaba-com-formato-virtual.ghtml

Galvão, A., Castro, B., Krein, J. D., & Teixeira, M. O. (2019). Reforma Trabalhista: Precarização do Trabalho e os Desafios para o Sindicalismo. *Caderno CRH, 32*(86), 253–270. https://doi.org/10.9771/ccrh.v32i86.30691

Gandra, A. (2020). Percentual de famílias com dívidas atinge recorde em março. Agência Brasil. *Agência Brasil*. Retrieved May 2020, from https://agenciabrasil.ebc.com.br/economia/noticia/2020-03/percentual-de-familias-com-dividas-atinge-recorde-em-marco

Ganz, L. C. (2020). A reforma das relações sindicais volta ao debate no Brasil. *Estudos Avançados, 34*(98), 127–142. https://doi.org/10.1590/s0103-4014.2020.3498.009

Gerhardt Lermen, N., & Picolotto, L. E. (2020). Trabalho rural, representação classista e lutas por direitos na produção de maçãs em Vacaria. *Revista Da ABET, 19*(1). https://doi.org/10.22478/ufpb.1676-4439.2020v19n1.52355

Hodson, R. (1991). The active worker: Compliance and autonomy at the workplace. *Journal of Contemporary Ethnography, 20*, 47–78.

Hodson, R. (2001). *Dignity at work*. Cambridge University Press.

Holmes, S. (2013). *Fresh fruit, broken bodies: Migrant farmworkers in the United States*. University of California Press, ProQuest Ebook Central.

Horton, S. B. (2016). *They leave their kidneys in the fields: Illness, injury, and illegality among U.S. farmworkers*. University of California Press.

IBGE. (2021). Desemprego recua para 13,9% no 4° tri, mas taxa média do ano é a maior desde 2012. *Agência IBGE Notícias*. https://agenciadenoticias.ibge.gov.br/agencia-noticias/2012-agencia-de-noticias/noticias/30130-desemprego-recua-para-13-9-no-quarto-trimestre-mas-e-o-maior-para-o-ano-desde-2012

Krein, J. D. (2018). O desmonte dos direitos, as novas configurações do trabalho e o esvaziamento da ação coletiva: consequências da reforma trabalhista. *Tempo Social, 30*(1), 77–104. https://doi.org/10.11606/0103-2070.ts.2018.138082

Leal, O. F. (2021). *Os gaúchos: cultura e identidade masculina no pampa*. Tomo Editorial.

Levesque, C., & Murray, G. (2006). How do unions renew? Paths to union renewal. *Labour Studies Journal, 31*(3), 1–13. https://doi.org/10.1177/0160449X0603100301

Longo, I. (2021, February 21). Bolsonaro reduz verba para combate ao trabalho escravo em mais de 40%. *Revista fórum*. https://revistaforum.com.br/direitos/bolsonaro-reduz-verba-para-combate-ao-trabalho-escravo-em-mais-de-40/

Martins, C. (2021, March 17). RS tem média de 22 resgates de pessoas em situação similar ao trabalho escravo por ano. *Zero Horas*. https://gauchazh.clicrbs.com.br/economia/noticia/2021/03/rs-tem-media-de-22-resgates-de-pessoas-em-situacao-similar-ao-trabalho-escravo-por-ano-ckmcbuilb0051016un60dzmyc.html

Martins Rodrigues, L. (1990). *Partidos e Sindicatos*. Ática.

Máximo, W. (2020, June 26). *Programa de redução de salário preserva 11,7 milhões de empregos*. Agência Brasil. https://agenciabrasil.ebc.com.br/economia/noticia/2020-06/programa-de-reducao-de-salario-preserva-117-milhoes-de-empregos

Maybury-Lewis, B. (1994). *The politics of the possible: The Brazilian rural workers' trade union movement, 1964–1985*. Temple University Press.

Mazon, E. (2020, March 5). Cesta básica fica 13,89% mais cara em 12 meses. *Zero horas*. https://gauchazh.clicrbs.com.br/economia/dicas-de-economia/noticia/2020/03/cesta-basica-fica-1389-mais-cara-em-12-meses-ck7e0j4jr01ie01pqqxxllbwt.html

Mendes, R. J. M., & Werlang, R. (2014). Suicídio no Meio rural no Rio Grande do Sul. In Á. R. Crespo, C. G. Bottega, & K. V. Perez (Eds.), *Atenção à saúde mental do trabalhador: sofrimento e transtornos psíquicos relacionados ao trabalho*. Evangraf.

Motta, G. (2019). Trabalho Assalariado e Trabalhadores Indígenas nos Pomares de Maçã no Sul do Brasil. *Unpublished doctoral dissertation*. Instituto de Filosofia e Ciências Sociais, Universidade Federal do Rio de Janeiro.

Müller-Jentsch, W. (2004). Theoretical approaches to industrial relations. In B. Kaufmann (Ed.), *Theoretical perspectives on work and the employment relationship*. IRRA Series.

Noronha, E. G. (2000). O modelo legislado de relações de trabalho no Brasil. *Dados, 43*(2). https://doi.org/10.1590/S0011-52582000000200002

Oliveira, C. V. (2020). Análise de mudanças da cobertura e uso do solo no Bioma Pampa com matrizes de transição. *Unpublished Dissertação de mestrado*. Universidade Federal do Rio Grande do Sul. http://hdl.handle.net/10183/217492

Ortmann, G. (1995). *Formen der Produktion: Organisation und Rekursivität*. Westdeutscher Verlag.

Peck, J. (1996). *Work-place: The social regulation of labour markets*. The Guilford Press.

Pickens, C., & Braun, V. (2018). 'Stroppy bitches who just need to learn how to settle'? Young single women and norms of femininity and heterosexuality. *Sex Roles, 79*(7-8), 431–448. https://doi.org/10.1177/0891243209340034

Picolotto, E. L. (2014). A formação de um sindicalismo de agricultores familiares no Sul do Brasil. *Sociologias, 16*(35), 204–236. https://doi.org/10.1590/S15174522201400010008

Picolotto, E. L. (2018). Pluralidade Sindical no Campo? Agricultores Familiares e Assalariados Rurais em um Cenário de Disputas. *Lua Nova: Revista de Cultura e Política, 104*, 201–238. https://doi.org/10.1590/0102-201238/104

Pierson, P. (1998). *Beyond the welfare state. The new political economy of welfare*. Polity Press.

Plassat, X. (2015). Campanha nacional da CPT contra o trabalho escravo. https://www.cptnacional.org.br/publicacoes/noticias/trabalho-escravo/2634-cpt-30-anos-de-denuncia-e-combate-ao-trabalho-escravo

Pontoni, G. A. (2016). Capacidad de negociación colectiva en Argentina, 1991–2011: La experiencia reciente del gremio camionero. *Revista de Ciências sociais, 29*(39), 131–154.

Rachelle, I. (2015). Assalariados rurais têm federação própria. Informativo de Imprensa Fetag n. 1089. http://fetagrs.org.br/assalariados-rurais-tmfederao-prpria/
Repórter Brasil. (2020). Trabalho escravo e gênero: Quem são as trabalhadoras escravizadas no Brasil? In N. Suzuki (Ed.), *Escravo, nem pensar*. Repórter Brasil.
Ribeiro da Costa, L. A. (2019). A estrutura sindical e a negociação coletiva brasileira nos anos 2000 e os primeiros impactos da Reforma Trabalhista (Lei 13.467/17). *XVI Encontro nacional ABET*. Salvador (BA).
Rodrigues, I. J., & Ladosky, M. H. G. (2015). Paradoxos do sindicalismo brasileiro: a CUT e os trabalhadores rurais. *Lua Nova: Revista de Cultura e Política, 95*, 87–142. https://doi.org/10.1590/0102-6445087-142/95
Rodrigues, O. K., Fleischmann, R. U., & Ferreira dos Santos, A. A. (2019). Subnotificação de Acidentes do Trabalho com Morte no Estado do Rio Grande do Sul em 2016: Discrepâncias das Estatísticas Previdenciárias Oficiais. *Revista Escola Judicial do TRT4, 1*(1), 151–180.
Saraiva, A., & Peret, E. (2019, March 30). Desemprego sobe para 12,7% com 13,4 milhões de pessoas em busca de trabalho. *Estatísticas Sociais*. Retrieved January 7, 2021. https://agenciadenoticias.ibge.gov.br/agencia-noticias/2012-agencia-de-noticias/noticias/24283-desemprego-sobe-para-12-7-com-13-4-milhoes-de-pessoas-em-busca-de-trabalho
Sayer, R. A. (1992). *Method in social science: A realist approach*. Psychology Press.
SEPLAG. (2021). Desigualdades de gênero dos ocupados com atividades ligadas à agricultura no RS. *Relatório Técnico*. Governo do Estado do Rio Grande do Sul. Departamento de Economia e Estatística. Retrieved November 17, 2021, from https://www.estado.rs.gov.br/estudo-do-dee-spgg-aponta-desigualdade-de-genero-nas-atividades-ligadas-ao-campo-no-rs?fbclid=IwAR1aqHnqs16M0vnr0Kdh_4wsZroHd7SS9M-hRXTpcT_ekLsDTL5riHxRlok
Silva Neto, B., & Basso D. (2015). *Os sistemas agrários do Rio Grande do Sul: análise e recomendações de políticas*. Ijui, Editora Unijuí.
Souto Maior, J. L., & Severo, V. (2017). *Manual da Reforma Trabalhista: Pontos e Contrapontos*. Editora Sensus.
Strauss, A., & Corbin, J. (1998). *Basics of qualitative research: Grounded theory procedures and techniques* (2nd ed.). Sage.
Vannini, P. (2019). *Doing public ethnography. How to create and disseminate ethnographic and qualitative research to wide audiences*. Routledge.
Viero, C. M., Camponogara, S., Cezar-Vaz, M. R., da Costa, V. Z., & Beck, C. L. (2016). Sociedade de risco: o uso dos agrotóxicos e implicações na saúde do trabalhador rural. *Escola Anna Nery., 20*(1), 99–105. https://doi.org/10.5935/1414-8145.20160014
Vollmann, W. T. (2007). *Poor people*. Ecco.

Index

A
Assistance services, 21, 22, 56, 72

B
Bancada Ruralista, 78
Bolsonaro, Jair, 20, 23, 27–30, 38, 57, 65, 66, 75, 78–80

C
Cadastro Geral de Empregados e Desempregados (General Register of Employment and Unemployment) (CAGED), 9, 30, 31, 46, 68
Carteira de trabalho (labor book), 17, 20, 22, 45
Central Única dos Trabalhadores (CUT), 41, 58
Class identity, 10, 16–24, 81
Collective bargaining, 1, 3, 4, 9, 10, 37–39, 42, 45–48, 50, 51, 54, 56–57, 61, 62, 64, 72, 76, 79, 80

Comparative analysis, 71
Confederação Nacional dos Trabalhadores Assalariados e Assalariados Rurais (National Confederation of Male and Female Rural Salaried Workers) (Contar), 21, 28, 30, 34, 39
Consolidation of Labor Laws (CLT), 37, 39, 75, 76
Contractual clauses, 2, 9, 42, 63, 70
Coverage (collective agreement coverage), 81
COVID-19, 1, 57, 62–64, 76

E
Estância, 2, 15, 35

F
Family farming, 10, 40, 41, 44, 58, 61, 66, 68, 79, 80
Fazendeiros, 6, 8, 10, 18, 22–26, 28, 34, 43, 51–54

Federação da Agricultura do Estado do Rio Grande do Sul (Federation of Agriculture of the State of Rio Grande do Sul) (Farsul), 22, 35, 41, 43, 45, 46, 48, 63, 66, 67, 79, 80

Federação dos Trabalhadores Assalariados Rurais no Rio Grande Sul (Federation of Rural Salaried Workers in Rio Grande Sul) (Fetar), 24, 25, 28–30, 40–48, 51, 55, 58, 62–65, 67–70, 80

Federação dos Trabalhadores na Agricultura Familiar (Federation of Workers in Family Farming) (Fetraf), 40, 41, 43, 47, 48, 55

Federal Police, 32, 33, 83

I

Imposto sindical (union tax), 9, 38
In-depth interviews, 8
Informal labor, 29, 30, 81

L

Labor reform, 2, 4, 6, 9, 26–28, 38, 39, 46, 50, 52, 57, 76, 80
Labor representation, 10, 39, 62, 79–83

M

Medical services, 22, 58, 59
Methodology, 10, 16
Ministry of Labor, 27–29, 42, 44, 46, 55, 62, 73, 75, 77
Multiple correspondence analysis, 9, 47–49

O

Obra social, 72–74

P

Pampa, 15, 16, 18, 30, 47, 48, 69, 71, 74
Pesticides, 6, 28, 29, 31, 32, 41, 42, 80–82
Planalto, 7, 15, 30, 41, 46, 47
Political lobbying, 78
Public ethnography, 8

Q

Quilombo, 19, 20

R

Rio Grande do Sul, 1–7, 9, 10, 15–19, 24, 25, 30, 32–35, 39–41, 43–47, 51, 54, 57, 59, 61, 62, 65, 68, 70–72, 74, 79–83
Rural worker, 2, 3, 5, 6, 8–10, 16–27, 30–33, 35, 40–42, 46, 47, 51, 53, 55–57, 61, 62, 64–67, 69, 72, 73, 79, 80
Rural workers' unions, 2, 3, 6, 7, 15, 25, 39, 40, 42, 54, 61, 62, 64–66, 81, 83

S

Safety at work, 3, 24–30
Service unionism, 57, 61
Sindical (single trade union principle), 37, 42, 43, 54, 68

Sindicato eclético (eclectic union), 33, 43, 64, 79
Sindicato pelego (yellow union), 3
Sindicato ruralista (employers' union), 8, 23, 45, 48, 49, 54, 55, 67–69, 79
Sindicatos, 3, 4, 8, 9, 18, 21–23, 25–27, 33, 35, 37, 40–43, 45, 47, 50–52, 55–57, 61, 62, 65, 66, 68–70, 74, 81
Slave labor, 10, 18, 35, 77, 78, 82

T
Temer, Michel, 75, 79, 81
Theoretical contributions, 3–6, 10

U
Unicidade, 37
Union representation, 9, 30, 58, 67, 69, 80, 81

W
Workplace accidents, 24

Printed in the United States
by Baker & Taylor Publisher Services